AFRICAN LIBERATION THEOLOGY

AFRICAN LIBERATION THEOLOGY

Intergenerational Conversations on Eritrea's Futures

Ghirmai Negash
&
Awet T. Weldemichael

THE RED SEA PRESS
TRENTON | LONDON | NEW DELHI | CAPE TOWN | NAIROBI | ADDIS ABABA | ASMARA | IBADAN

THE RED SEA PRESS
541 West Ingham Avenue | Suite B
Trenton, New Jersey 08638

Cover art: Ermias Ekube
Book and cover design: Lemlem Taddese

Library of Congress Cataloging-in-Publication Data

Names: Negash, Ghirmai, author. | Weldemichael, Awet Tewelde, author. | Catholic Church. Catholic Bishops of Eritrea. Where is your brother?
Title: African liberation theology : intergenerational conversations on Eritrea's futures / Ghirmai Negash & Awet T. Weldemichael.
Description: Trenton : The Red Sea Press, 2018. | Includes bibli ographical references and index.
Identifiers: LCCN 2017056940| ISBN 9781569025864 (hardback ; al kaline paper) | ISBN 156902586X (hardback ; alkaline paper) ISBN 9781569025871 (paperback ; alkaline paper) | ISBN 1569025878 (paperback ; alkaline paper)
Subjects: LCSH: Church and state--Eritrea. | Liberation theolo gy--Eritrea. | Catholic Church--Eritrea. | Catholic Church. Catholic Bishops of Eritrea. | Catholic Church--Pastoral letters and charges. | Social justice--Eritrea--Religious aspects. | Social justice--Reli gious aspects--Catholic Church. | Church and social problems--Er itrea. | Church and social problems--Catholic Church. | Postcolo nialism--Eritrea.
Classification: LCC BX1682.E65 N44 2018 | DDC 282.635--dc23
LC record available at https://lccn.loc.gov/2017056940

TABLE OF CONTENTS

INTRODUCTION

Among many traditional African societies, those in present-day Eritrea included, individuals and groups had clear, if negotiated, recourse to redress grievances. Their traditions permitted victims of – and witnesses to – injustice to call on elders, traditional authority and religious leaders to intervene. The same social norms made it imperative for these traditional and religious authorities to at least intercede on behalf of the injured and the weak. Consistent with this tradition, Fr. Gebreyesus Hailu, the earliest Eritrean and African novelist, lamented the silence of his community's religious leaders in the face of colonial injustice. In a little known 1927 novel that was brought back to life and wider circulation in translation as *The Conscript*, Fr. Gebreyesus is appalled at the wretchedness of Eritrean colonial troops fighting their colonizers' wars against fellow Africans, and laments, "Our priests, why don't you speak out?".

Failing that, individual members or groups took the law into their own hands, although such actions rarely spread so widely as to render the society chaotic. Collectively dubbed as *shiftenet* (literally, banditry, hence *shifta* for a bandit) in Northeast Africa, resistance against traditional authority, even violent retribution against traditional office holders, has a long history. Before the end of the first decade of the 20th century, the overwhelming brute force and ruthlessness of the various colonial rulers suppressed these tendencies to rebel against authority and largely undermined traditional mechanisms of justice. By the second half of the century, the anticolonial parties broke through repressive colonial apparatuses and mobilized the popular urge for justice. The armed anticolonial revolutionaries intensified the liberatory mobilization of the African masses. Popular loyalty to the nationalist cause and the pursuit of nationalist ideals mushroomed. The people directly participated in the independence war through active involvement in associations of peasants, workers, youth, women, and other groups.

The history of the African postcolonial landscape is far from uniform, as different independent states have made different choices with differing results. The record of successes and failures also differs not only between countries but also within the same country contingent on the successive governments that held power after independence. That said, it is fair to say that, as a collective, the postcolonial ruling elite have fallen grotesquely short in the implementation of the nationalist aspirations for and promises of democratic governance, administration of justice, and the respect of human rights. That seems to be especially the case in the postcolonies that decolonized through protracted armed struggles.

Having effectively mobilized the masses, the revolutionary anticolonial elite of the movements appeared to be ambivalent toward the empowered masses that lent them maximum support. Within the pervading context of war, the movements had quickly instituted rigid mechanisms of monitoring, regulation, and discipline. Coming on the heels of a long period of colonial terror, the nationalist regimes of revolutionary discipline proved to be antithetical to the democratic ideals of the African anticolonial revolution, and imperiled empowerment of the people. Once decolonization was achieved, the mechanisms and platforms that rallied the masses around the national liberation movements were disbanded, and, in many cases, replaced with apparatuses of harsh repression. Such regimes of order and discipline also foreclosed traditional mechanisms of redress for injustice.

For far too many decolonized Africans, the struggle for complete liberation had to continue. While the full account of the recent and ongoing domestic struggles against homegrown tyranny across Africa waits to be written, this book deals with contemporary issues at the crosshairs of faith and politics in the Horn of Africa nation of Eritrea. It grapples with questions of injustice, as well as traditional non-religious and religious avenues of appeal for redress in what has become an archetypal post-colony in the 21st century.

The former Italian colony of Eritrea, in Northeast Africa, gained de facto independence in 1991 after a protracted armed struggle against Ethiopian domination that had annexed the country following the departure of Italian colonizers and a decade-long British rule. Eritrea's independence was formalized in 1993 with a 98.5 percent vote for independence in an internationally observed referendum. Since independence, however, consequences and boomerangs of ill-thought-out government policies have marred Eritrea's domestic affairs and its relations with regional and international powers. Gross human rights violations and intense surveillance and repression characterize the state's disposition toward its citizens. Meanwhile, citizen responses have been marked by complacency, complicity, general apathy, and resistance in the form of defiance and, ultimately, massive flight from the country. These dynamics have rendered the state a faltering shadow of itself and careened the country to the edge of the precipice.

Indeed, today's Eritrea is beleaguered by internal oppression (and regional and international alienation) and widespread violation of basic rights and freedoms of citizens in the absence of the rule of law and the pervasive militarization of society. This profoundly negative situation has triggered ongoing waves of human migration and has impacted Eritreans living outside the country as well. The Eritrean government and its apologists swing between denying these ugly truths and imputing them to adversaries, internal and external. Old and new voices of reason, and both novel and traditional opposition constellations have been instrumental in critically analyzing the situation and educating the public through radio, print, and digital communications. The new generation of refugees and exiles has been especially active in resisting adverse political developments in the country they left behind.

Traditional and religious institutions also have proved that they do not always grovel in submission during dangerous times or in the face of egregious violations. On the country's 21ˢᵗ anniversary of formal independence, the four bishops of the Eritrean Catholic Church compiled the last of a long list of their critical interventions in the country's spiritual, sociopolitical, cultural, and economic life. Released to the public in May 2014 under an evocative title, "Where Is Your Brother?", the pastoral letter painstakingly documented the tragic conditions in which the Eritrean people continue to live under the government's heavy hand and the citizens' neglect of their responsibilities. The spirit, text, and dissemination of the document mark important historical pointers – perhaps even a watershed – in the ongoing discussions about Eritrea's current dire state and possible futures. The heated discussions and debates that "Where Is Your Brother?" generated in various media outlets speak to its unequivocal significance.

Shortly after the letter's release, Ghirmai Negash offered a widely read and influential Tigrinya-language commentary titled, "The Priests Have Spoken: Beginnings of Liberation Theology in Eritrea?".

Initiating his critique with a discussion of Gebreyesus Hailu's *The Conscript* as a starting point, he shows the historical and inter-generational connections between Hailu's text and the Bishops' pastoral letter. The essay also unpacks the deeper thematic connections of the pastoral document with the original conceptions of Liberation Theology, and reflects on the prospects of immediate and long-term uses of the Latin American concept as adopted in the African postcolonial setting. Inspired and anchored by both the 2014 pastoral letter and Negash's treatise, Awet T. Weldemichael continues the intergenerational dialogue by engaging and building on Negash's analysis. He brings into sharper focus the significance, meaning, and ramifications of the Eritrean bishops' critical intervention as rooted in the longer history of evolving Catholic social teachings.

This volume consists of four chapters that place "Where Is Your Brother?" in its proper historical and contemporary context. In the first and third chapters, Weldemichael adds to the conversation on the relevance of the bishops' message and the putative power of Liberation Theology in Eritrea. Responding to Negash's original intervention, in the first chapter, he furthers the analysis by surveying the long history of Catholic social teachings and the church's advocacy for social justice within the context of faith groups in African and Eritrean settings. In seeking answers to how Eritrea got into its current predicament in the first place, he examines in the third chapter the dichotomy between the means and outcomes of the struggle for liberation in Eritrea against the backdrop of an African anticolonial ideology and praxis, and lived experiences in the African postcolony. The English translation of Negash's original article ("The Priests Have Spoken: Beginnings of Liberation Theology in Eritrea?") appears in the second chapter.[1]

The book concludes with a fourth chapter by Negash in which he draws on Pan-Africanist visionary legacies to grapple with the provocative but fundamental question of who Eritreans are and who they desire to be – in their own view. Based on an analysis of literary and cultural texts, he argues that the country's historical predicament of isolation and alienation demands the development and nurturing of a critical culture of self-scrutiny and openness as a means to undo internal oppression and international isolation. The first three chapters are interconnected and speak to each other in the strict sense of the word. The fourth chapter diverges from and is loosely connected to

---

1   Translation by Ghirmai Negash. All translations that appear in the chapters are by the respective authors of the chapters.

the others. We believe this is both a weakness and strength of the book. We had agreed that the fourth chapter would be written deliberately to go beyond mere critical analysis, to open conversations that can help coming to terms with contemporary and future problems of Eritrea.

As co-writers of this book, we should explain a few points to our readers at this point. This book has been long in the making. Since late 2014, we have had numerous long, highly stimulating exchanges by telephone and email. Because the project demanded more intensive interaction, we had to meet twice, once in Athens, Ohio in summer 2016, and a second time in Woodbridge, Virginia, in summer 2017. Sustained by our dedication to the project, both meetings involved candid and heated debates, introspection of our deeply held convictions and perspectives, and a critical reflection on our respective aspirations and possible avenues of their realizations. Not only has that experience been rewarding to both of us individually, but we believe it also has enriched the book while retaining individual authorial responsibility for – and voice in – the chapters. It goes without saying that we welcome healthy debates around the topics we have broached and constructive criticism of the perspectives and analyses we have presented.

Finally, such a project cannot succeed without active moral and material support of many. Several of our respective colleagues and students either read some of these chapters or tuned in to our exchanges to offer valuable feedback. We cannot mention all of them, but we cannot pass without especially thanking Dr. Nazareth Amlesom (at the University of Bergen), Abraham T. Zere (at Ohio University) and Samuel Emaha (at Makerere and Queen's). We also want to thank Ohio University graduate student Jerry Gaba, and Fullbright student Oumarou Abdoulaye Balarabe for their assistance with the bibliography. We extend our sincere gratitude to Margarite Grootjes and Professor Steve Howard for critically reading the whole manuscript and offering constructive feedback throughout. We thank Terry Smith for his skillful and meticulous copyediting of the manuscript. We also would like to express our profound gratitude to Semere Habtemariam for his permission to reprint in this book his English translation of "Where Is Your Brother?", and to Ermias Ekube for his generosity in painting the front cover of the book. We would like to recognize the friendship and most cooperative relationship we have had with our publisher, Kassahun Checole of The

Red Sea Press. He inspired and kept encouraging us to write this co-authored book, with his unwavering belief in the success of the project. We thank both of our families for their tremendous patience and the sacrifices that they made during our travels for this book. We especially thank Margarite, Sarah, and Rosa in Ohio, and John, Natsinet, and Japheth in Virginia for their incredible hospitality and most pleasurable moments during the writing experience. During our entire stays, they tolerated our long, heated, and loud exchange of views into the wee hours. Farris Awet was born when we were finalizing the current book; we welcome his arrival into the family and celebrate Miriam's incredible patience and support throughout the pregnancy and into the early postnatal weeks.

Ghirmai Negash & Awet T. Weldemichael
September 2017

THE CATHOLIC CHURCH: A LONE VOICE?

Chapter One

Awet T. Weldemichael

> The coming of the kingdom of God is not something that can be observed, nor will people say, 'Here it is,' or 'There it is,' because the kingdom of God is in your midst.
> —*The New Testament*, Luke 17:21-22.
> "Feed my lambs...Take care of my sheep."
> —Jesus to Peter in *The New Testament*, John 21:15-17.

In May 2014, the Eritrean Catholic Church offered sobering reflections on the root causes and dynamics of the prevailing dire conditions in Eritrea. Signed by Eritrea's four Catholic bishops/eparches and titled "Where Is Your Brother?", the apostolic message triggered great interest and revived enlivened discussions among Eritreans about the tragic state of affairs in their country. Some Eritreans welcomed it as a breakthrough coming out of the church against government actions and inactions. Others looked askance at what they considered to be an intrusion of a religious institution in politics, following a streak of prior disapprovals and even condemnations.

Eritrean mathematician and political commentator Professor Ghidewon Abay Asmerom, for example, had sternly remarked in late 2013 that priests should solely concern themselves with spiritual matters. In a powerful oratory on Eritrean national identity, he was unforgiving in his condemnation of religious leaders' involvement in politics. He recited an Eritrean proverb to scold what he branded as "swearing priests" for seemingly engaging in self-contradiction,[1] before admonishing,

> Those of the world should occupy themselves with worldly matters. Those of the spirit should concern themselves with spiritual matters. Spirituality teaches love, redemption, honesty, and harmony; not something else. However, if, instead of mediating between God and man, you are out to trade the people and the foundations of the nation and its identity, then it becomes a matter that concerns all Christians and Moslems, as well as people like me; and there is no joke about it. Because many innocent [citizens] have sacrificed for this nation, we challenge and condemn any campaign that comes in the name of religion, and it is certain that we will defeat it, and render it unsuccessful.[2]

After citing a verse from the Bible foretelling signs of the end of time, Asmerom concluded, saying, "If the evil enter to preach in the church and mosque pretending to be holy, we have to be able to soberly identify them as deceiving wolves in sheep's clothing, and not having or carrying God's spirituality and righteousness."[3]

---

1   The full proverbial expression in Tigrinya reads: *"ቀሽን መሓልን፤ ጕሓላን ስዓልን፤ ኖኼዕን መስተርን፤ ንሳን ሓካልን ክሰማዕዕ አይከኣልን።" ፕሮፈሰር ጊዶዎን አባይ፤ "መሰረት ህዝብን ሃገርን ንምድዋን ብሽም ሃይማኖት ዝግበር ዘሎ ፍንፉንን ርኹስን ጠቓናዊ ጎስጓስ፤"* speech delivered in Washington, DC, on December 8, 2013. Available at: https://www.youtube.com/watch?v=HML4dOqXorc (Last accessed on August 1, 2017).

2   The Tigrinya text reads as follows: *"ናይ ዓለም ኮይኑ ናይ ዓለም ይገብር። ናይ መንፈስ እንድሕር ኮይኑ ኸአ ናይ መንፈስ ይገብር። መንፈስ ከአ ፍቅርን ጽድቅን ቅንዕና ስኒትን እምበር ካልእ አይመሃርን'ዩ። አብ ሞንን አምላኽን አብ ሞንን ሰብን ኬንካ አብ ክንዲ ተዓርቆ፤ ህዝብን መሰረት ሃገርን መንነትን ክትሽይጥ እንድሕር ኬንካ ግን፤ ንክርስትያን ይምልከቶ፤ ንሶላማይ ይምልከቶ፤ ንኸምዚ ከማይ. . . ውን ይምልከቶ ስለዝኾነ ብሃገር ጸወታ የለን። እዚ ሃገር'ዚ ሓላላት ዝተበጀዉሉ ሃገር ስለዝኾነ ብሽም ሃይማኖት ዝመጽእ ጎስጓስ ንምክቶ ንኹንኖ፤ ከም ንስዕሮን ከምነፍሽሎን ከአ ርግጽ'ዩ።"* Ibid.

3   The Tigrinya text reads as follows: *"ርኹሳት ቅዱሳት መሲሎም አብ ቤት መቕደስ አብ መሳጊድ አትዮም እንተ ሰበኹ፤ ናይ ምትላል ቆኹሉ ከለዉ አጎዛ በጊዕ ዝለበሱ እምበር ናይ ሓቂ ናይ ቅድስናን ቅንዕናን ናይ አምላኽ [ዘይ]ምኻት አርጢብና ከነልብዮም ክንክእል አለና።"* Ibid.

The Eritrean Catholic Church's pastoral letters, however, would not be the first time that leaders of a religious community, on their own initiative or in response to the urgings of their members, interceded for or championed the worldly preoccupations of their followers. When natural and/or man-made disasters overturn their world, people tend to turn to and seek emotional solace – and even physical protection – in bigger power(s) and their spiritual guidance. Africa is no stranger to people following their spiritual leaders into the course of action that the latter prescribed in facing challenges. During the early violent encounters between African peoples, on the one hand, and European colonial intruders, on the other, the former often followed their spiritual leaders to political action. From Sheikh Abdulkadir in Algeria to the Maji Maji leaders in Tanzania and the spirit mediums among the Shona and the Ndebele in Zimbabwe, African spiritual leaders led their followers to resist foreign domination. Similarly, in apartheid South Africa, churches and church leaders helped articulate the cause of liberation and served as important launching pads for the liberation movement.

Although historically Liberation Theology has been identified with the Catholic Church in Latin America, different faith groups have opposed oppression and advocated the right to freedom of their followers and non-followers alike. From such a secular point of view, one can plausibly argue that the pursuit of social justice lies at the heart of both Christianity and Islam. Opposition to oppression (foreign or domestic) often drew inspiration from the Bible or the Qur'an, and was as often framed in the language of these holy books. It is, therefore, hardly surprising that the articulate young Eritrean Quranic reciter in Jeddah, Sheikh Tawfeeq al-Sayegh, among many others, recently personified Islam's position on the fair treatment of all human beings and social justice. In a string of powerfully moving Friday sermons between 2013 and 2014 that later earned him deportation from the Kingdom of Saudi Arabia, not only did Sheikh Tawfeeq condemn the violence that was being perpetrated by Muslims on Muslims and non-Muslims alike, but he also vehemently denounced as un-Islamic the treatment of foreigners in his adopted abode.[4]

---

4   Whereas several of Sheikh Tawfeeq's sermons (on distribution of material wealth, charity, fair treatment of all human beings …etc) have periodically been uploaded on YouTube, the most moving one on violence and the quest for justice and among his last sermons before he was deported from Saudi Arabia in August 2014 (in spite of his residence

Politically in Eritrea, both Islam and Christianity nurtured local nationalism in their own unique ways, if at times discordant; but Eritrean nationalism always formed the basis for their direct participation in and active advocacy for the nationalist cause. Islam, for example, played an important role in crystalizing Eritrean nationalism by gluing together disparate pro-independence interests since the defeat of Fascist Italian domination during World War II.[5] Emperor Haile Selassie ceaselessly courted and ultimately succeeded in winning over some prominent Eritrean Muslims to his scheme of incorporating Eritrea with Ethiopia. In spite of that, however, not only did Eritrean Muslims pioneer the armed struggle for independence but Islam helped draw attention to the plight of the Eritrean people and their cause. Narrow-minded elements within the independence movement sought to use it in destructive ways in the form of a nation-wide Islamist agenda, but they were overcome as much by secular Muslims as by those of Christian background.

Similarly, in spite of Emperor Haile Selassie's manipulation of administrative ties of the Eritrean Orthodox Church to its Ethiopian counterpart to sway the former toward supporting his unionist project, lay Orthodox Christians and many members of the clergy progressively opposed and fought against union with Ethiopia. While some priests and deacons quietly supported the struggle for independence in different ways, including secretly housing independence fighters or passing on valuable information, others joined the ranks of independence fighters and actively fought – and died fighting – against Ethiopian domination.

Most prominent among Orthodox clergy's resistance was Abuna Philipos (the first Orthodox Patriarch of Eritrea between 1996-2002) when he was head monk of the Bizen Monastery (Debre Bizen). He had openly sympathized with the Eritrean resistance movement since the 1970s and occasionally met with its ranking leaders in secluded locales. In the mid-1980s, he reportedly resisted Dawit Welde Giorgis's

---

there for most his life) can be heard here: https://www.youtube.com/ watch?v=j28fIc6yciI. This sermon, in which, among other things, he condemns the August 2013 massacre of supporters of the deposed Muslim Brotherhood in Cairo, is presented as proof of his support to the brotherhood that the Saudi royals opposed and reason for his deportation.

5   Joseph L. Venosa, *Paths toward the Nation: Islam, Community, and Early Nationalist Mobilization in Eritrea, 1941–1961* (Athens, OH: Ohio University Press, 2014).

(the then Ethiopian governor of Eritrea) urging of Eritrean elders to call on their children, i.e. the independence fighters, to surrender, after which he was banished to Ethiopia and did not return to Eritrea until after independence. He went on to become the first patriarch of Eritrea's Orthodox Church separate from Ethiopia's – with the backing of the country's new president, Isaias Afwerki.

Before the advent of modern education and secularism, religious leaders constituted the main traditional intellectuals in Eritrea, interpreting the worldly and spiritual realms surrounding them to their following and conceptualizing the people's practices for the outside world to understand. Eritrean priests and sheikhs proved to be reservoirs of inherited wisdom and accumulated practical knowledge both of which were then passed on to subsequent generations. Nevertheless, the religious institutions and traditional intellectuals incrementally withdrew from the public sphere in the face of the onslaught of European colonialism and modern intellectualism. In the 20th century, modern Eritrean intellectuals (some with strong footing in church education) largely dominated the interpretation of local and foreign concepts to their people, while also theorizing about the varied local experiences and making them comprehensible to each other and to the outside world. Yet, religious-cum-traditional leaders retained their customary roles within the confines of their groups be it religious or secular, only occasionally making their presence openly felt in the broader national public sphere.

The May 2014 pastoral letter, "Where Is Your Brother?", is one such intervention that helped prompt Ghirmai Negash's analysis of the prospects of Liberation Theology in Eritrea, and that forms the basis of this book. The limited research and data on recent and ongoing intercessions of the Eritrean mosques and (other) churches on behalf of citizens limit the scope of this chapter to the Catholic Church. It will, therefore, confine itself to analyzing the Vatican encyclicals that serve as bases for the Catholic Church's involvement in the worldly affairs of mankind and the Eritrean Catholic Church's critical interventions on the sociopolitical and economic affairs of the Eritrean people since independence.

Catholic Social Teachings from the Holy See to Eritrea

The Catholic Church is no different from the other faith-based groups that protested the persecution or oppression of their followers and non-followers alike. In spite of its longest tradition of aligning with state officialdom and power, including the "Just War" doctrine,

11

colonialism and slavery, the church gradually developed social teachings that advocated for the worldly liberation of its laity (parallel to their spiritual redemption), i.e. freedom from poverty, ignorance, and political oppression during one's human life. In the past century and half, it has proven as much a leader as an adept follower in the promotion of much-needed reforms in human society. At the onset or not long after major milestones in modern history (often tragic or with tragic consequences), the Holy See made consequential interventions on the socioeconomic and political conditions of its laity as well as everyone else's. These are the encyclicals that constitute the normative and substantive foundations of Catholic Social teaching and can be considered long harbingers of Liberation Theology in Latin America as well as the Eritrean bishops' important document, "Where Is Your Brother?".

Laying the ground for the first such encyclical in 1891, Pope Leo XIII dispelled the Church's neutrality on the plight of mankind thus: "Neither must it be supposed that the solicitude of the Church is so preoccupied with the spiritual concerns of her children as to neglect their temporal and earthly interests. Her desire is that the poor, for example, should rise above poverty and wretchedness, and better their condition in life; and for this she makes a strong endeavor."[6]

Although some found Leo XIII's message suspect and others were offended by it, "even among Catholics," as Pope Pius XI later pointed out, the Church continued its critical examination of sociopolitical and economic conditions of the world, and accordingly adjusted its ways of handling them within the parameters of its spiritual mission.[7] Many of its subsequent reflections on the earthly life of human society were similarly couched. In 1961, for example, Pope John XXIII asserted the Church's position on the earthly conditions of human beings thus: "Though the Church's first care must be for souls, how she can sanctify them and make them share in the gifts of heaven, she concerns

---

6   "Rerum Novarum: Encyclical of Pope Leo XIII on Capital and Labor," 1891. Last accessed August 1, 2017. http://www.vatican.va/holy_father/leo_xiii/encyclicals/documents/hf_l-xiii_enc_15051891_rerum-novarum_en.html

7   "Quadragesimo Anno: Encyclical of Pope Pius Xi on Reconstruction of the Social Order," 1931. Last accessed August 1, 2017. http://www.vatican.va/holy_father/pius_xi/encyclicals/documents/hf_p-xi_enc_19310515_quadragesimo-anno_en.html

herself too with the exigencies of man's daily life, with his livelihood and education, and his general, temporal welfare and prosperity."[8]

Forty years after Pope Leo XIII's precedent-setting encyclical, Pope Pius XI reinforced his predecessor's apprehension about socialism and also cautioned against unbridled capitalism. Although the political ideological leanings of the Catholic Church in the late 19th century (or even in the 21st century for that matter) can be debated, Pius XI called for the reconstruction of a societal order on the basis of social justice:

> To each, therefore, must be given his own share of goods, and the distribution of created goods, which, as every discerning person knows, is laboring today under the gravest evils due to the huge disparity between the few exceedingly rich and the unnumbered propertyless, must be effectively called back to and brought into conformity with the norms of the common good, that is, social justice.[9]

As the world was still reeling out of the dislocations of World War II and former colonies started to gain independence, Pope John XXIII issued two important encyclicals (in May 1961 and May 1963) that focused on the worldly aspect of human life as well as among nations. Convinced that "it is no less necessary – and justice itself demands – that the riches produced be distributed fairly among all members of the political community," he exhorted in 1961 that developed nations give altruistic technical and financial aid to the less developed ones lest they be "introducing a new form of colonialism – cleverly disguised, no doubt, but actually reflecting that older, outdated type from which many nations have recently emerged. Such action would, moreover, have harmful impact on international relations, and constitute a menace to world peace."[10] The pope emphasized the need to spread

---

8 "Mater et Magistra: Encyclical of Pope John XXIII on Christianity and Social Progress," May 15, 1961. Last accessed August 1, 2017. http://www.vatican.va/holy_father/john_xxiii/encyclicals/documents/hf_j-xxiii_enc_15051961_mater_en.html

9 "Quadragesimo Anno: Encyclical of Pope Pius Xi on Reconstruction of the Social Order," 1931. Last accessed August 1, 2017. http://www.vatican.va/holy_father/pius_xi/encyclicals/documents/hf_p-xi_enc_19310515_quadragesimo-anno_en.html

10 "Mater Et Magistra: Encyclical of Pope John XXIII on Christianity and Social Progress," May 15, 1961. Last accessed August 1, 2017.

and assimilate the Church's social doctrines "and put into effect in the form and manner that the different situations allow and demand," but forewarned about the difficulty of putting them into effect. Subsequent developments on the ground proved him right.

In spite of such groundbreaking internal philosophical innovations and progressive doctrinal guidelines, the Catholic Church around the world continued to embrace the capitalist state and retained a fixed hostility toward progressive political ideas and movements of the oppressed fringes of the human society. It was within this context that the ideas of Liberation Theology seeped from the grassroots up to the highest echelons of the Church in Latin America in the late 1960s – after Vatican II.[11] Based on an astute observation of the rampant poverty of the many vis-à-vis the preposterous plenty of the corrupt and oppressive few, and influenced by Marxism as well as the emerging theories of development and underdevelopment, Peruvian theologian Gustavo Gutiérrez advocated for a theology of liberation premised on the preferential treatment of the poor. Fr. Gutiérrez went on to co-author the 1968 document of the Conference of Latin American Bishops that condemned the sociopolitical and economic inequalities across Latin America. That document held that the principles of Vatican II would be best implemented through "a distribution of resources and apostolic personnel that effectively gives preference to the poorest and most needy sectors…"[12] In resolving to stand for justice and in defense of the defenseless, Latin American bishops declared in Medellín:

> We ought to sharpen the awareness of our duty of solidarity with the poor, to which charity leads us. This solidarity means that we make ours their problems and their struggles, that we know how to speak with them. This has to be concretized in criticism of injustice and oppression, in the struggle against the intolerable situation

---

http://www.vatican.va/holy_father/john_xxiii/encyclicals/documents/hf_j-xxiii_enc_15051961_mater_en.html

11   "Gaudium Et Spes: Pastoral Constitution on the Church in the Modern World," December 7, 1965. Last accessed August 1, 2017. http://www.vatican.va/archive/hist_councils/ii_vatican_council/documents/vat-ii_cons_19651207_gaudium-et-spes_en.html

12   Latin American Bishops "Poverty of the Church" Medellín, Colombia, September 6, 1968. Last accessed August 1, 2017. http://www.povertystudies.org/TeachingPages/EDS_PDFs4WEB/Medellin%20Documen t-%20Poverty%20of%20the%20Church.pdf

which a poor person often has to tolerate, in the willingness to dialogue with the groups responsible for that situation in order to make them understand their obligations.[13]

Many Latin American Catholic priests paid a heavy price for doing so. Known for his advocacy on behalf of the downtrodden and against the widespread human rights violations in El Salvador, Archbishop Oscar Romero of San Salvador was assassinated in March 1980 at the very altar where he had just finished saying mass in front of the whole congregation.[14]

The pioneer liberation theologian's subsequent articulations and admonishments of the Church to introduce a "preferential option for the poor" initially irritated the Vatican. One of Fr. Gutiérrez's vigorous critics was Cardinal Joseph Ratzinger (future Pope Benedict XVI) who was the Vatican's principal for doctrinal affairs between 1981-2005.[15] Nevertheless, not only did the Vatican fall short of condemning the

---

13 Latin American Bishops "Poverty of the Church" Medellín, Colombia, September 6, 1968. Last accessed August 1, 2017. http://www.poverty studies.org/TeachingPages/EDS_PDFs4WEB/Medellin%20Documen t-%20Poverty%20of%20the%20Church.pdf

14 Julian Miglierini, "El Salvador Marks Archbishop Oscar Romero's Murder," BBC, March 24, 2010. Last accessed August 1, 2017. http://news.bbc.co.uk/2/hi/8580840.stm

Although many hail Romero as a hero of Liberation Theology, his former personal secretary recently stated that the archbishop was neither a liberation theologian nor inspired by it. Instead, the former secretary claimed, he followed the Second Vatican Council and "called for a personal encounter with Christ Jesus, which implied a preferential option for the poor, because Jesus opted for the poor to save us all." See Alvaro de Juana, "Archbishop Romero had no Interest in Liberation Theology, says Secretary," Catholic New Agency, February 21, 2015. Last accessed August 1, 2017. http://www.catholicnewsagency.com/news/archbish op-romero-had-no-interest-in-liberation-theology-says-secretary-79788/

15 Cardinal Joseph Ratzinger, "Liberation Theology: Preliminary Notes," August 6, 1984. Last accessed August 1, 2017. http://www.christendom-awake.org/pages/ratzinger/liberationtheol.htm

This document is considered to be "private" reflections of the cardinal predating the Holy See's official position on Liberation Theology, in which Cardinal Ratzinger was instrumental. See "Congregation for the Doctrine of the Faith: Instruction on Certain Aspects of the "Theology of Liberation," August 6, 1984. Last accessed August 1, 2017. http://www.vatican.va/roman_curia/congregations/cfaith/documents/rc_co n_cfaith_doc_19840806_theology-liberation_en.html

Dominican friar; it also integrated key tenets of Liberation Theology into its catechisms that were articulated by none other than Cardinal Ratzinger himself during John Paul II's pontificate. Gutiérrez's and the Medellín declaration of Latin American Bishops entered the long list of Catholic pontiffs, thinkers and encyclicals whose teachings informed the Church's social doctrines that were latterly enunciated in its catechisms.[16]

On the recommendation of Church leaders convoked on the 20th anniversary of Vatican II, in 1986 Pope John Paul II established a commission of cardinals chaired by Ratzinger to compose "a catechism or compendium for all Catholic doctrine regarding both faith and morals."[17] Nearly a decade worth of extensive work culminated in the release of *Catechism of the Catholic Church* in 1994 that serves as a key reference for the Church's social teachings parallel to explications of its doctrines and the spiritual journey of the faithful. In it, the Church ruled out a direct role in politics and social organization.[18] Nevertheless, not only did it call for social justice within nations and justice and solidarity among them, but it also expressed *"preferential love"* (emphasis original) for the poor for whose "relief, defense, and liberation" the Church has worked.[19] Moreover, it retained its prerogative to "make a moral judgment about economic and social matters, 'when the fundamental rights of the person or the salvation of souls requires it'."[20] Although the Catholic Church has had various roles in many historic injustices around the world and helped legitimize others, the above preoccupations have also persisted, with the life, words and actions of Pope Francis, its current pontiff, best epitomizing its positive interventions in the transient affairs of mankind.

This is the broader doctrinal and historical backdrop to the Eritrean Catholic Church's crucial interventions in the Eritrean sociopolitical milieu at least since the end of the independence war. The Church reflected on the country's socioeconomic and political conditions through numerous interjections it made on occasions it deemed significant enough for its voice to be heard. Catholic bishops

---

16 Gustavo Gutiérrez, *A Theology of Liberation* (Maryknoll, NY: Orbis Books, 1973).
17 *Catechism of the Catholic Church* (New York: Doubleday, 1997), 2-3.
18 Ibid., 646 (paragraph 2442).
19 Ibid., 648 (paragraph 2448).
20 Ibid., 641 (paragraph 2420).

released statements of consolation to the public and made calls on their laity, all Eritreans and their leaders. Much of these went unnoticed by the broader public because of government crackdown on independent Catholic media outlets in the mid-1990s, and also because the Church did not wish them to receive wider circulation than they did – lest the government perceived them as challenging state authority and reacted to them accordingly.

"Where Is Your Brother?" is only the latest of such pastoral messages, and Ghirmai Negash did a commendable job of not only making this important document more easily accessible to its readers, but also in placing it within its proper local and global context. His analysis is in line with the long tradition of Eritrean intellectuals reflecting on the fate of their people and helping chart out their future. Whereas being intellectual is relative and the contribution of Eritrean intellectuals toward their people's welfare is long, one can plausibly begin with the Eritrean Catholic theologian, Dr. Gebreyesus Hailu, whose 1927 piece of literary work is considered among the first of its kind in African history.[21] During the formative years of Eritrean nationhood, political leaders doubled as their country's thinkers and intellectuals by dint of their limited (advanced in the Eritrean setting) education within a largely illiterate society that lacked any institution of higher learning. The Eritrean movement for independence (both the activist and the armed) featured a wide array of intellectual capital that helped articulate the key issues of their times, as well as of the past and future within regional and global context, a herculean undertaking that waits to be recognized and celebrated.

In line with this intellectual tradition but without any sense of presumption, Negash took it upon himself to help Eritreans, in general, and those who have read "Where Is Your Brother?" in particular, to understand the document in question within its unique local historical and global context. The leadership of Eritrea's spiritual and intellectual leaders – as displayed in the Catholic bishops' pastoral document and Negash's analysis, respectively – will be much needed in the times to come as Eritrea confronts its challenges and charts its future. A critical analysis and understanding of the past, especially with regard to how we got here in the first place, will be helpful in grappling with current and future opportunities and challenges.

---

21 Gebreyesus Hailu, *The Conscript*, trans. Ghirmai Negash (Athens: Ohio University Press, 2013).

Speaking Truth to Power from the Pulpit/Minbar

In Eritrea, state relations with the churches and mosques are governed by Proclamation 73/1995 of July 1995. In the absence of an overarching regime of the rule of law, this restrictive proclamation has so far enabled the state to aggressively intervene – or ceaselessly try to – in the affairs of Eritrea's religious institutions, throwing them into confusion and at times even paralysis. Since independence, the state has placed a firm grip on the two biggest religious communities, i.e. Orthodox Christians and Muslims, so as to command their undivided and absolute loyalty and devotion. State security personnel also penetrated and placed a stranglehold on the religious institutions as if they were preempting potential rivals and threats. In the face of this state onslaught, Eritrean churches and mosques have visibly been struggling to find their respective internal balance and manage their intercourse with the state. Much research is needed to document their inner dynamics, their respective interactions with the state as well as with each other, and their advocacy for the rights of their members and the broader Eritrean public.

Among many serious issues, the Eritrean Islamic Awqaf, for example, has bitterly protested the government's refusal to restore confiscated property of the mosque and its management. So has the Orthodox Bishopric Council. In a long running contest, in early October 2014 six Eritrean monasteries (of the Orthodox Church) publicly ejected two officials that the government had appointed to run church affairs. Many other smaller churches also have had issues with one or another government policy, action, or inaction. The Seventh Adventist Church, the Jehovah's Witnesses, and other smaller faith groups have been forced to close their doors. In light of a paucity of data, however, and because this chapter concerns itself with the May 2014 document of Eritrea's Catholic bishops, the subsequent analysis will center on the Catholic Church that seems to have fared better by dint of its sophistication and autonomy, which at least partially emanates from its organic organizational and doctrinal ties with the Holy See.

The limited available data seems to indicate that since Eritrea's days of highest pride and glory, through its agonizing descent to Eritreans' current state of disgrace and humiliation, the Catholic Church may have been the lone institutionalized voice of reason, restraint, and social justice. It has consistently spoken truth to power. Although its voice drowned in the deafening silence surrounding its apostolic messages and its regular missives to the government, the

Church seized every opportunity to officially protest the state's heavy hand in dealing with the Church, the people and their civic institutions. To those who are privy to Catholic social teachings (briefly outlined above) in general and more specifically to the Eritrean Catholic Church's record since independence, "Where Is Your Brother?" does not come as a surprise. Nevertheless, under the current grim circumstances in Eritrea and viral social media around the world, the euphoria following its release is as understandable as Ghirmai Negash's analysis is much needed and timely.

In 2008, the Eritrean Catholic Church published a compilation of all of its apostolic messages, communications to the government and President Isaias Afwerki, as well as other documents released to its laity and the Eritrean public.[22] The book was produced to inform the clergy, and it remained in limited circulation first because of general government clampdown on Catholic media outlets since the mid-1990s, and second because the Church chose to prevent its messages from being misconstrued as oppositional canvassing against the government. I will here limit my treatment to the two major apostolic messages (of 1991 and 2001) that preceded "Where Is Your Brother?", as they resonate with the quest for the rule of law and social justice in Eritrea today.

In its first post-liberation pastoral message of July 1991, the Eritrean Catholic Church related life in the preceding years to actual and metaphorical death and compared post-liberation Eritrea to the dead bones that the mighty hand of God brought back to life in the prophesy of Ezekiel.[23] According to the Church, sincere thanks were due to God for He similarly breathed life into Eritreans by making military victory possible in May 1991. Peace, however, was not the mere end of war, for it required cautious, sustained, and methodical development of all facets of the individual members and the society at large. Convinced that the empowerment of the individual does not conflict with – but in fact reinforces – the interests of the collective, the bishops argued that the state of the human person reflected the

---

22 ካቶሊካውያን ጳጳሳት ኤርትራ, *መንግድታቱ አቻኦ: ሐዋርያዊ መልእኽታትን ሰነዳትን (1991– 2007)* (Bologna: Editrice Missionaria Italiana, 2008). The entire book and individual messages/documents within it are also translated into English in the same publication as Catholic Bishops of Eritrea, *Making God's Ways Straight: Pastoral Letters and Documents (1991 – 2007)*.

23 *The Old Testament*, Chapter 37.

success of the country's developmental programs.[24] A society's structures and institutions should accordingly aim to meet the rights of the individual to material and non-material needs. Ignoring these rights, the bishops warned, "would mean that man will become the servant of those same social structures and functions. To build a society that afflicts man rather than blesses him would appear to be a contradiction in terms!".[25] The inauguration of a healthy society that is based on unity and reconciliation thus rests on "fundamental inner renewal of persons" that in turn follows from the development of a holistic person.[26] The essentials of this chain of positive developments stumbled from the start and ultimately fell by the wayside as the dream of the immediate post-independence years turned into a nightmare before the turn of the decade.

In their 2001 apostolic message, the Catholic bishops went straight to the heart of the matter asking rhetorically if Eritrea had been truly liberated during the preceding decade of independence, i.e. whether it had produced liberated citizens, and whether Eritreans had been worthy of it.[27] While recognizing the successes of the pro-rural, pro-poor policies in education, healthcare, and expansion of infrastructure, they bleakly reflected on what had gone on since independence: restrictive economy, directives from above that were often divorced from the reality on the ground, a rudimentary justice system that could breed corruption, meager wages that could not sustain the national servicemen/servicewomen, a deliberate attack on and deterioration of

---

24 *"ሰላምን ምዕብልናን፡ ብዝተሓደሰ መንፈስ ንሓዳስ ኤርትራ። ሓዋርያዊ መልእኽቲ ንምእመናን ንኹሎም ሰብ ጽቡቅ ድላይን፤"* ሓምለ 1991 ዓ.ም.ፈ. in *መንገድታቱ አቐኖዉ, ገጽ* 25 or *Making God's Ways Straight,* 25.

25 *Making God's Ways Straight,* 199. The Tigrinya version in page 26 reads thus: *"ብእንጻሩ ነዛን መሰላት'ዚኣተን ሸለል ምባል ማለት፡ ንሰብ ናይ'ቲ መሳርዓትን ተግባራትን (ምንቅስቓሳትን) ባርያ ወይ ግዙእ ምግባሩ ማለት እዩ። ስለ'ዚ ከዓ እቲ ዝህነጽ ማሕበረሰብ ምእንቲ ረብሓ ሰብ ዘይኮነስ፡ ኣንጻር ሰብ ይኸውን፤ ባዕልኽ ንባዕልኽ ምጥፋእ ማለት እዩ።"*

26 *"ሰላምን ምዕብልናን፡ ብዝተሓደሰ መንፈስ ንሓዳስ ኤርትራ። ሓዋርያዊ መልእኽቲ ንምእመናን ንኹሎም ሰብ ጽቡቅ ድላይን፤"* ሓምለ 1991 ዓ.ም.ፈ. in ካቶሊካውያን ጳጳሳት ኤርትራ፤ *መንገድታቱ አቐኖ:, ገጽ* 25.

27 *"ነዛ ሃገር እግዚኣብሔር የፍቅራ ኢዩ።* ሓዋርያዊ መልእኽቲ ኣብ 10ይ ዓመት ናጽነት፤" 24 ግንቦት 2001 ዓ.ም.ፈ. in ካቶሊካውያን ጳጳሳት ኤርትራ፤ *መንገድታቱ አቐኖ, ገጽ* 83.

historic cultural assets, and finally the destructive war with Ethiopia. In a lengthy, sophisticated treatise, they called for reconciliation and forgiveness within an orderly regime of rule of law that protected human rights, tolerated diversity, and promoted the holistic development of the person with a special attention to that of women.[28] In light of the more than decade-long tragedy that has plagued Eritrea with the flight of its youth and their agonizing plight afterwards, the bishops' May 2001 message regarding the youth is especially worthy of mention. Sternly warning that the country was anticipating the return of the young who had just endured the physical and psychological traumas of the brutal war, the bishops rhetorically asked, "What are our youth thinking and saying today? How do they view their country? Do they trust the administrative system? Does the country's economic development and social and religious stability give them cause for hope?", and went on to prophetically answer:

> If hope has evaporated, then they have no future to look to at home, and it is only obvious that they will look for solutions elsewhere. They will simply abandon their mother country and will look for a better future abroad. A nation that is unable to harness the potential of its youth is doomed to instability. Indeed its very existence as a country may be put into question. We believe that we, as both civic and religious leaders, have a great responsibility to bear. There is no point in just asking, "Why are our youth choosing to go abroad?" – for no-one leaves a country of milk and honey, as the saying goes, to seek another country offering the same opportunities. If one's homeland is a place where peace and freedom are enjoyed and employment is available, there is no reason to leave it to endure exile, loneliness and hardships of all kinds.[29]

---

28 Ibid., ገጽ 84 – 107.

29 "God Loves This Country: Pastoral Letter on the Occasion of the 10th Anniversary of Independence," 24 May 2001 in Catholic Bishops of Eritrea, *Making God's Ways Straight*, 255-256.
The Tigrinya version is as follows: "ኣብቲ ዚህነጽ ምምሕዳራዊ ስርዓትን፣ ኤኮኖሚያዊ ምዕባለን፣ ማሕበራዊ ድሕነትን፣ መንፈሳዊ ሰረትን ኩሉ ተስፉ ዚህብ ምልክታት እንተዘይ ረኺቡሞሉ ናይ መጻኢ ዕድሎምን ሕይወቶምን ጸልማት ኮይኑ ኪራኣዮም፣ ንዝተወልዱላ ሃገር ራሕሪሖም ከኣ መንጎዲ ስደት ከማዕድዉ ናይ ግዲ እዩ። ሓይሊ ንኡስ ወለዶ ዝይብላ ሃገር ከኣ መጻኢ ሃለዋታ ኣብ ሓደጋ ወዳቒ ማለት እዩ። . . . ስለምንታይ መንእሰያትና ዓድናን ዘግዕድዉ ምባል ትርጉም ኣይህልዎን። ዓዲ ሰላም: ዓዲ ፍትሒ:

Besides such extended apostolic documents, the Eritrean Catholic Church also offered critical messages at important turning points in post-independence Eritrea. Although reconciliation remained a running theme through all of their major apostolic messages, the bishops made a separate appeal in August 2001 that "A Spirit of Reconciliation and Unity was Needed."[30] In the immediate aftermath of the government's internment of the entire student body of the University of Asmara and in the midst of the climaxing tension within the top government leadership, the Church urged the leaders to find a negotiated resolution to their differences: "We believe that negotiation and mutual understanding are the only" avenues to a solution without losers were the Eritrean family to remain united.[31]

Not only did many Eritreans, collectively and individually, similarly call for a conciliatory resolution of the simmering dispute within the leadership, but also appealed for national reconciliation. Lamenting the failure to go through a process of national reconciliation immediately after independence, a group of 13 Eritrean scholars and professionals (the G-13) believed that the opportunity had not been lost permanently and appealed in October 2000 for the government to extend a "call for reconciliation… to all Eritreans irrespective of belief or political affiliation."[32] At least one group of Eritrean elders attempted to reconcile the two factions of post-

---

ዝመስለካ ዓው ኢልካ እትዛረበላን፤ ሰራሕካ እትሓድረላን ዓዲ ምስ ሓዝካ፤ መዓር ገዲፉ መዓር ዘናዲ ስለዘየልቦ፤ ንስደት ክንዲ ዘግዕድዉ ዝኸዱን፤ ካብ ስደት ዝምለሱን ዝውሕዙን መንእሰያት ከሀልዉና ናይ ግዲ እዩ።" "ናዛ ሃገር እግዚኣብሔር የፍቅራ እዩ:- ሓዋርያዊ መልእኽቲ ኣብ 10ይ ዓመት ናጽነት።" 24 ግንቦት 2001 ዓ.ም.ፈ.፤ ኣብ ካቶሊካውያን ጳጳሳት ኤርትራ፤ መንገድታቱ ኣቦና, ገጽ 108-109።

30 "መንፈስ ዕርቅን ምውህያድን የድሊ:- ለበዋ ንሕዝብን መንግስትን ኤርትራ" ነሓሰ 2001 ዓ.ም.ፈ. in ካቶሊካውያን ጳጳሳት ኤርትራ፤ መንገድታቱ ኣቦና, ገጽ 127–129.

31 "መንፈስ ዕርቅን ምውህያድን ድሊ.፤" Berhane Magazine, ነሓሰ 2001 ዓ.ም.ፈ. Also reproduced in ካቶሊካውያን ጳጳሳት ኤርትራ፤ መንገድታቱ ኣቦና, ገጽ 127–129.

32 Variously referred to as "Berlin Manifesto" or "the G-13 letter," the document that they sent to the Eritrean president is now available in the public domain. Also reproduced as "Letter to H.E. Isaias Afwerki," Berlin, October 3, 2000, in Bereket Habte Selassie's *Wounded Nation: How a Once Promising Eritrea was Betrayed and its Future Compromised* (Trenton, NJ and Asmara: The Red Sea Press, 2011), Appendix I, 289-296 [here 292].

independence leaders. Subsequent attempts at reconciling the two sides were restricted to individuals – although prominent – using their proximity to the president to appeal to him personally. Over time, the voices of reconciliation drowned in the rising cacophony of opposition politics and activism that, among others, stipulate the unconditional removal of the president and hold him and his close associates personally responsible for all of Eritrea's ills.

Conclusion: National Reconciliation and Political Reawakening

Surely, such a tragic turn of events as has been seen and experienced in post-independence Eritrea cannot be entirely relegated to the failings or malice of a single person or group – whatever their weaknesses. Nor can the impediments to change be miniaturized to a single individual and/or group. Whereas the principal hurdle to long-term stability will be the absence of such a leadership, i.e. vacuum, a bottomless abyss that is no longer a remote hypothetical probability, the key to national salvation will be for all Eritreans to take their respective shares of responsibility.[33] Because citizens of any country ought to take the blame or earn the acclaim for the system that presides over their country for so long (two and half decades and counting in the case of Eritrea). It is high time that Eritreans seek each other's forgiveness and reconcile, get in touch with the core Eritrean values that made independence possible in the first place and reawaken the long-stalled pluralist political programs through inclusive processes.

Spurring the articulation of Catholic social doctrine with his historic encyclical of 1891, Pope Leo XIII offered the following words of wisdom that are as pertinent to Eritrea today as they were to the strife ridden world following the industrial revolution:

> When a society is perishing, the wholesome advice to give to those who would restore it is to call it to the principles from which it sprang; for the purpose and perfection of an association is to aim at and to attain that for which it is formed, and its efforts should be

---

33 Whereas Yemen, Libya and Syria are ongoing examples, I am a firsthand witness from the ground in Somalia to the dire consequences of similar processes 20 years on. Resisting my cautioning against such prospects, many fellow citizens succumb to the same old rhetoric of Eritrean exceptionalism when in fact Eritreans are as exceptional in their own ways as are all other peoples in their respective ways.

put in motion and inspired by the end and object which originally gave it being.[34]

At the heart of the decades-long political and armed struggle in Eritrea was a righteous quest for peace, dignity, liberty, and prosperity at home, and justice and equality in the region and the world. It was an arduous process that saw generations of Eritreans putting their lives on hold, completely dedicating themselves to the cause of liberating their people and overcoming a myriad of internal challenges that followed the contours of Eritrean social-cultural cleavages as much as ideological and personal proclivities. Although not without its consequential pitfalls, the armed struggle is a heroic tale of young and old men and women jumping in front and into the fray, and making the ultimate sacrifices for their people's right, dignity, and freedom. It is a proud and humbling legacy of sacrifices that subsequent generations of Eritreans readily took on and paid for with numbing courage and selflessness. Every Eritrean has a solemn duty to honor the martyrs and rally in defense and promotion of their value: courage, selflessness, and unity – all in pursuit of full liberation from fear and want.

The sacrifices of the Eritrean people, their continued commitment to the ideals of the liberation struggle, and their future good demand serious and dignified deliberations on how to bring the country back on track toward a better future. At a time of fast deteriorating conditions on the ground that are testing Eritrea's historic social harmony, the only avenue left for national salvation is an all-inclusive process of reconciliation. This is an essential steppingstone toward a participatory political system governed by the rule of law. Just as the voices for change in Eritrea need more unifying principles than their shared desire to see the government in Asmara removed from office, so too does the government need to appreciate that staying the course is just as hazardous and accordingly take urgent measures. For the process as well as the outcome of national reconciliation to be enduring, it has to include all threads of the social, cultural, political, and historical fabrics that constitute Eritrea.

---

34 "Rerum Novarum: Encyclical of Pope Leo XIII on Capital and Labor," 1891. Last accessed August 1, 2017. http://www.vatican.va/holy_father/leo_xiii/encyclicals/documents/hf_l-xiii_enc_15051891_rerum-novarum_en.html

	THE PRIESTS HAVE
Chapter	SPOKEN: BEGINNINGS
Two	OF LIBERATION
	THEOLOGY IN
	ERITREA?

THE PRIESTS HAVE SPOKEN: BEGINNINGS OF LIBERATION THEOLOGY IN ERITREA?

Chapter Two

Ghirmai Negash

> "Our priests, why don't you speak out?"
> —Gebreyesus Hailu, *The Conscript*, 26.

Introduction

This essay was inspired by the pastoral letter issued in May 2014 by the bishops of the Catholic Church of Eritrea, under the title, "Where Is Your Brother?". Authored by the four highest Catholic priests in the country, this document has been circulating through the internet and social media outlets within the country and internationally for some time, generating heated debate and discussion. The text provides a vivid picture of the social, economic and political crises and confusion plaguing the country and its five million people, as a result of the dictatorial system led by unelected President Isaias Afwerki. This essay, "The Priests Have Spoken: Beginnings of Liberation Theology in Eritrea?", is intended to provide my observations and questions to interested readers about "Where Is Your Brother?". The idea is to continue the discussion and encourage exploratory research. While I focus on the singular significance of "Where Is Your Brother?" as a new theoretical intervention of emancipatory and moral concept, my analysis will posit that this document also constitutes a special precedence in the Eritrean context for two main reasons. First, from a critical viewpoint, the text offers a nuanced and detailed analysis of, in the authors' thematization, the "oppression, suffering, and cries"[1] of the Eritrean people since independence. No other document from within the country thus far has put forth such meticulous, candid, and rhetorically sophisticated depiction of the prevailing conditions in Eritrea. Second, in addition to its detailed and careful portrayal of the realities on the ground, "Where is Your Brother?" distinctively invokes the language, thought, and practice of Liberation Theology prevalent among Latin American Catholic churches. Initially developed by priests and intellectuals on that continent, Liberation Theology provided substantial help in giving voice to and aiding the struggles of the disenfranchised populations in Latin America. When considered in the Eritrean context, a critical reading of the pastoral letter, "Where Is Your Brother?", raises important conceptual questions, especially in light of its force and connections with the Latin-America born theology: Is the emergent explicit intervention of the Catholic Church of Eritrea merely a transitory phenomenon, or does it herald the birth of Liberation Theology as a serious, long-term movement in the country?

Even though the analytical part of this essay will discuss it in more detail, a brief explanation of the title, "The Priests Have Spoken", is warranted. It evokes Gebreyesus Hailu's powerful quote, "*Our priests, why don't you speak out?*". As Hailu's readers may recall, the quote appears in his fine Tigrinya-language novel, *The Conscript*, that was originally written in 1927 and published in 1950 (trans. 2013). There is a saying in Tigrinya that roughly translates into English as "one thing leads to another". When I read the Catholic pastoral letter, it reminded me of those words from Hailu's novel. Beyond the linguistic connections, there is also substantive overlap between Hailu's narrative and the document of the four Catholic bishops. Hailu, like the bishops, was a highly educated Catholic priest. His book forcefully condemns the Italian colonial rule of his time in Eritrea, the harsh conditions of military conscription of those times, and the colonial conspiracy to prolong its rule by dividing and pitting Africans against one another. The critical approaches both in *The Conscript* and in "Where Is Your Brother?" call for a conjoined reading and examination of the two texts. This is because, with both rooted in

---

1   See Appendix. "Where Is Your Brother?". Translation by Semere Habtemariam. Last accessed August 1, 2017. http://awate.com/pastoral-letter-a-complete-and-literal-translation/

Catholic moral foundations of social justice, they equally condemn the oppression of Eritreans and advocate for their rights and dignity. This essay is divided into four sub-sections as follows. I start with a subsection titled *"The Conscript* and Historical (Re-)iterations" in order to explore the historical and thematic significance of the novel, *The Conscript,* and its relationship with current conditions in Eritrea. I then establish the historical and thematic connections of Hailu's novel with the bishops' "pastoral letter" in the subsection titled "From *The Conscript* to 'Where Is Your Brother?'". Following that, I present two consecutive subsections titled "Liberation Theology in Latin America" and "Liberation Theology in Eritrea?". Liberation Theology is a new concept in the Eritrean context. As a result, the discussion will necessarily be exploratory and geared toward its relevance in the country.

The Conscript and Historical (Re-)Iterations

In 1927, Dr. Gebreyesus Hailu, an Eritrean Catholic priest, wrote a historical novel about the Italian colonial possession of Eritrea and its people. Father Hailu (1906-1993) had a PhD in theology, and according to theorist and cultural critic Laura Chrisman, he was one of the great thinkers of his time, whose "approach to colonialism anticipates the midcentury thinkers Frantz Fanon and Aimé Césaire [and like them] highlights the dehumanization at the core of colonial domination".[2] Since the period of Italian colonial rule and until his passing, Hailu was a dedicated spiritual and community leader who provided spiritual and social services to his communities in Eritrea and Ethiopia. At some point he was also a vicar general of the Catholic Churches in the two countries. As previously mentioned, although he wrote the book, *The Conscript,* at a young age in 1927, it was not published until 1950.

Against the backdrop of the military, political, religious, social, and psychological changes brought about by Italian colonialism in Eritrea, the book depicts the transition of Eritrean society from its traditional African modes of life at the turn of the 20th century to what Terence Ranger referred to as European-invented modernity under the violent auspices of European conquest.[3] The novel focuses on the traumatic

---

2 Laura Chrisman, Introduction to *The Conscript* by Gebreyeus Hailu (Athens: Ohio University Press, 2013), xviii-xix.

3 Terence Ranger, "The Invention of Tradition in Colonial Africa," in *Perspectives on Africa: A Reader in Culture, History, and Representation,* eds. Roy

dark years of Eritrean history known to Eritreans as "the era of the Tripoli Campaign" or in Tigrinya *"Zemen Tribuli"*, an era of colonial military campaigns in Libya. In the campaign, Eritrean conscript soldiers were forced to fight against their fellow African brothers in Libya, on behalf of the Italian colonial expedition.

On top of his native African education, Hailu was European educated. Despite his associations with the Italian administration, he was keenly aware of the vicious Italian colonial intentions in Eritrea. As the preface to his novel makes clear, his critical thinking had enabled him to closely follow and thoroughly examine the colonial designs behind the Tripoli campaign. Explaining his motives in writing a fictionalized account of Eritreans' harsh experience in Libya, he states:

> This book which is being printed under the title *A Story of a Conscript* reflects my impressions when, at the age of eighteen, I traveled by sea to Italy to seek an education. It is also about the memory of my fellow-countrymen, the *ascari* recruits, who were traveling overseas at the time. And that is why my writing is of a young person... I consider myself a blessed person and thank my God for enabling me to express the concerns and feelings of my people at that young age.[4]

The Conscript narrates the story of a protagonist named Tuquabo who took part in the Libyan expeditionary war with the Italian army. The book details the conscripts' long journey from Asmara to Libya. The journey's context and its malicious objectives are rendered in lucid language. Also vividly depicted are the hidden and explicit sentiments of the conscripts as they leave from the Ferrovia Train Station in Asmara; the clamor and wailing of the families attending the conscripts' departure; and the harsh beating, "yes, with a whip like a donkey",[5] of the frenzied crowd by military police at the site. Likewise, the passage of the train through the tunnels, zigzagging train tracks, and panoramic hills surrounding the villages of Arberobue and Nefasit is rendered beautifully. Analogous passages further recount the arrival of the conscripts in the Eritrean port of Massawa at sunset, and portray

---

Richard Grinker and Christopher B. Steiner (Cambridge: Blackwell, 1997), 597-612.

4   Gebreyeus Hailu, *The Conscript* (Athens: Ohio University Press, 2013), xxix.

5   Ibid., 12.

the course of their journey to Libya, crossing the Red Sea, Port Sudan, and the Egyptian Suez Canal. Initially, the conscripts are filled with youthful bravado and are determined to make a name for themselves by going to the Libyan war. However, they do not find warfare as easy as they expected. The Eritrean *ascaris* not only experience the unfamiliar travails of journeying across sea and desert; they learn to their chagrin that the Libyans are militarily resilient and fully prepared to pay the ultimate sacrifice to defend the independence of their country and their human dignity as a people.

Before leaving for Libya, the Eritrean conscripts receive military training and imbibe anti-Arab propaganda. While Italian propaganda portrays the Arabs as uncivilized savages, it paints a glorious image of Italian power and fame. The Libyans, however, shatter the conscripts' preconceptions, forcing them to re-examine the stated objectives of the campaign, and to gradually start reassessing their own situation and that of their country. At this critical juncture, Tuquabo, the novel's main character, begins to scrutinize his situation and has a personal revelation. What was this self-knowledge for Tuquabo? For him, an answer to this question entails at least three things. Politically, Tuquabo develops a proper assessment of the war; he understands that European colonization of Africa is unjust and brutal; and he acquires an anti-colonial perspective. Moreover, realizing that Italian-inculcated education about Islam and the Arabs is poisonous racialist thinking, he corrects his prejudices against the Arabs and the Muslim faith. Finally, and most importantly, Tuquabo becomes aware of an ironic contradiction: the conscripts, like himself, were fighting to sustain the same imperial oppression that had colonized them and their people. He ends up strongly condemning the conscripts' participation in the Libyan war. He expresses his regret and self-criticism thus:

> [The Libyans] lacked guns and were short of ammunition. They didn't have a king or a chief to lead them. Even so they did their best to save their land from aliens. On the other hand, it was strange to watch the *Habesha*, who at first did nothing when their land was taken and bowed to the Italians like dogs (as if that was not shameful enough indeed), preparing to fight those Arabs who wanted to defend their country. The *Habesha* were fighting for those who came

to colonize and to make others tools of colonizing African neighbors, without anything of benefit to their country or society.[6]

In the subsequent two sections, the author movingly describes in detail some of the critical moments of the hideous war in the desert. Specifically, in the passages that chronicle battle scenes, some of the conscripts are dying of thirst; others simply scatter away, while still others are seen falling and rising as their bodies sink into the desert sand, to eventually be eaten by vultures. The author thus documents the horrific and sub-human conditions experienced by Eritrean *ascaris* during the war. He observes bitterly:

> A proverbial saying goes, 'There are times when fighting a war is easier than resisting hunger.' Pity the conscripts who were on the brink of death from thirst yet were guarding the tent for somebody who carried water. Nobody could understand how terrible it must have felt for those who needed to get a share of the water. They were like the rich man in hell who longed for a drop of water from Lazarus. They would have loved to get a taste of water from anyone. But they weren't there to privilege themselves by quenching themselves with water; they were supposed to stand there and prevent any other conscript from coming close to the tent. Whenever they heard the splash of water, their hearts would jump. It was exactly like watching a dog whose eyes, while one is eating, are raised and lowered following the movement of one's hand. They were, after all, like dogs, if you compared them with the Italians. In fact, dogs fared better; they at least ate their masters' leftovers.[7]

Shortly afterwards, the author expresses the grief brought on Eritrean families by the horrendous death of the conscripts in Libya. The riveting description employs language similar to that used following the tragic 2013 Lampedusa shipwreck and other atrocities and tragedies that have befallen the current generation of Eritrean youth.[8] Echoing the collective sorrow of the people, Hailu laments:

> They were inconsolable. Their loss was the more painful because also they were unable to claim the remains of their sons and loved ones. Not knowing whether the bodies were eaten by fish in the sea

---

6   Ibid., 29.
7   Ibid., 45-46.
8   This event took place on October 3, 2013. In this widely publicized catastrophe, at least 365 people were recorded dead.

or by vultures and hyenas in the desert drove their grief beyond imagination.[9]

Although many sections of *The Conscript* chronicle the dynamics of the war, the author also intermittently reverts to religious language beyond expressions of anger and frustration. In a calmer voice, he explains the helplessness of human beings in the face of such terrible calamity, and pleads with his God for mercy, and thus entrusts the conscripts' salvation to divine hands:

> [The conscripts] found the sand hotter as they dug deeper, and losing all their patience, they looked up to the sky and prayed to their God in despair, 'O All-seeing God, we are in distress.' A few among them (not only one or two) had patience and would try to calm down the rest but were out of words. How would it be possible to utter a word when the throat was dry and the tongue couldn't get any saliva?[10]

While Hailu, as a religious figure, believed that everything ultimately was in the hands of God, he, nonetheless, also reasons that humans have a role to play in determining the course of history and can be masters of their fate. He calls upon citizens of all nations to take full responsibility for their actions in bringing about social and political changes in their societies. Specifically addressing his community's priests and religious leaders, Hailu urges them not to fail in their duties as spiritual leaders and entreats them to speak out about the fate of the conscripts languishing in the Libyan desert. His message is encapsulated in the following lines of a traditional song: "Our priests, why don't you speak out? Not even one young man can be found; all have gone to Tripoli".[11]

There is a common saying that history repeats itself. Although historical iteration should be studied carefully case by case, Eritrean history has produced historical occurrences remarkably similar to each other. Conditions in present-day Eritrea recall the historical circumstances depicted in Hailu's novel as discussed above. Looking at the historical parallels in conjunction with each other rather than in isolation, the resemblance manifests itself in two ways. On the one hand, the flood of problems caused by successive wars, conscription,

---

9   Hailu, *The Conscript*, 54.
10 Ibid., 46.
11 Ibid., 26.

and repression have continued to plague the country and push its people into the emptiness of the desert and the calamities of the sea. On the other hand, like Gebreyesus Hailu's firm stand in publicly condemning Italian conscription during his time, the four bishops of the Catholic Church spoke out with similar courage and volume. They express their concerns and criticism about the appalling situation in Eritrea in the same critical tone as Hailu. In fact, the only substantial difference between Hailu's *The Conscript* and the four bishops' "Where Is Your Brother?" is that the former is a work of historical fiction and the latter a living testimony. *The Conscript* narrates the past suffering of Eritrean conscripts under Italian colonial rule, whereas "Where Is Your Brother?" bears witness to the ongoing suffering of the Eritrean people under the rule of President Isaias Afwerki.

From *The Conscript* to "Where Is Your Brother?"

As all interested readers must now recognize, "Where Is Your Brother?" is a document that emanates from the religious moral stance of the four Eritrean Catholic bishops, and delivers a thorough and objective analysis of the current Eritrean political situation. In articulating their concerns and what compelled them to write and distribute the document, the authors knit together vision and moral courage. They spell out their central motive in the following way:

> 'Men expect from the various religions answers to the unsolved riddles of the human condition, which today, even as in former times, deeply stir the hearts of men: What is man? What is the meaning, the aim of our life?' … The Church has the responsibility to shed light with the Gospel on the temporal and worldly affairs… Because 'The joys and the hopes, the griefs and the anxieties of the men of this age, these are the joys and hopes, the griefs and anxieties of the Church…' 'The light of faith is not to make us forget the suffering of this world', but it is faith 'that will guide us in the steps we take, and light that is needed in our journey.' … Based on the faith, 'that nourishes our lives daily and strengthens and encourages us anew'; it is our duty to consider our situation and the situation of our brother.[12]

Considering the current religious, ethnic, and regional sensitivities and divisions in Eritrea, the bishops strongly emphasize that they did not have any ill intentions or ulterior motives in writing the document.

---

12 "Where Is Your Brother?", Appendix, sections 11 and 9.

To that end, they state, "We embark on this task, not because we are interested in gaining worldly or temporal honor or faith, or to bring others into our fold, but by a genuine desire to serve."[13] In his article "Assessing the Impacts of Liberation Theology in Latin America," Daniel Levine, a liberation theology scholar, discusses at length the struggle of Catholic bishops for justice in Latin American countries. Levine's analysis of liberation theology in Latin America helps in discussing the Eritrean bishops' motivation, purpose, and vision, encapsulated in the pastoral letter. Levine says:

> [The Colombian priest's] comments point to a role for religion that transcends the institutional and ideological boundaries of formal church structures. They suggest that religion has a primary role to play in human liberation, and that in the search for liberation, transmitting the Gospel message of salvation cannot be separated from the creation of a better life, here and now.[14]

Levine further explains the core idea of liberation theology and its connections with the empowerment of the poor and underprivileged. He argues that "concern with poverty and the poor knits liberation theology together in theory and practice".[15] In the current situation of Eritrea, this means that the Church should not necessarily limit itself, but rather should act upon the social and economic edifices of the society and use its moral authority to oppose oppression and exploitation. When viewed from this perspective, the contents of "Where Is Your Brother?" corroborate Levine's conclusions.

The pastoral letter mainly seeks to discuss the current socio-political problems in Eritrea. The central themes of the document can be summarized as follows: Acknowledging Eritrea's wealth and resources, the bishops' letter discusses the peaceful co-existence and religious and ethnic tolerance of Eritrean society; it celebrates the long-standing tradition of cooperation and strong communal ties. It rejoices in the long-established Eritrean tradition of brotherly and sisterly care toward one another. However, while recognizing Eritrea's potential and especially its achievements after independence, the text doesn't recoil from describing the country's continued suffering and instability

---

13   Ibid., section 9.
14   Daniel H. Levine, "Assessing the Impacts of Liberation Theology in Latin America," *The Journal of Politics* 50, no. 2 (1988): 241.
15   Ibid., 243.

caused by unresolved issues and problems. The pastoral letter identifies the following as most pressing among them.

1. Recalling the recent tragedy in the Mediterranean Sea (off the coast of Lampedusa) that took the lives of 365 Eritrean migrants, the document discusses the causes of their exile and destruction. Arguing that the "tragedy was the culmination of all the suffering that has been inflicted by human traffickers, smugglers and human oppressors in the past years, in every mountain, valley, desert and sea", it calls on the Eritrean people not to succumb to the repeated challenges, disintegrate and lose their identity as a people. It instead encourages the people not to lose hope and forgo the idea of return.

2. Regarding the Eritrean exodus, the document explores different possible reasons. It argues that the main reasons were the lack of proper jobs and educational opportunities for the youth; the Eritrean government's inability to resolve the "no peace no war" situation with Ethiopia; and the fact that the majority of youth are stuck in military conscription. In their letter, however, the bishops took pains to avoid a biased analysis that only blames the government. They also placed some of the blame on young people for opting to flee into exile instead of working to improve their lot at home; waiting for remittances from abroad instead of seeking opportunities to improve their livelihood; and going abroad using fake marriages. These are among the factors that contributed to the large-scale flight from the country.

3. Human and organ trafficking is a recent brutal phenomenon that has greatly affected Eritreans. This ruthless act carried out by both nationals and foreigners involves rape and sodomy, bodily mutilation, and organ harvesting. The bishops express their grief at these inhuman acts and firmly condemn the trafficking that leads to them. Appealing to the international community and Eritrean government, they call for immediate action. In spite of the barbarity of the trafficking, the pastors appear intrigued by the indifference of the international community, in general, and the Eritrean government's cold reaction, in particular:

> What is troubling is ... the emergence of a phenomenon where people are kidnapped while seeking refuge and taken

hostage for lucrative ransom; man has become man's worst enemy; man, who has been created in the image of God, has been deprived of his dignity and rights when his organs are harvested to be sold in a black market. We have never heard of anything like this in history; when one sees the time of slavery and rule of the beasts making it in our advanced world; one is bound to ask if the conscience of the perpetrators has been desensitized, why it is that the world that is witnessing this is so tolerant? Why not the rush to condemn and confront it; particularly those places this inhumane and barbaric acts are taking place and those people who are committing the crime; and on those these things are committed under their watch…governments and leaders should not have spared any effort to thwart it!! Is it because our will has waned that this shocking practice is allowed to continue? Or our ability has been emasculated? Or if there is any exerted effort, is it because it has not borne any fruit? Or who is benefiting from this? What can we say?[16]

4. Regarding the socio-economic situation of Eritrea, the document states that the society is suffering from numerous diseases (including HIV/AIDS, hypertension, diabetes, and stress) that mainly result from poverty. In addition to climate change, increasing desertification, and land deterioration causing economic hardships, the country is suffering terribly from unemployment, brain drain, and mass migration. In addition to the youth, the pastors write, parents are joining their children into exile for family reunifications. If the trend continues, they fear that the country may be left without successor generations:

> [W]e are duly concerned by the far-reaching ramifications the continual exodus of refugees and the depletion of human capital will incur on the future of the country. It is true wherever a refugee settles s/he will always miss and long for his/her homeland; but truth be told that based on history the number of those who returned home is insignificant to merit counting. We are not only talking about the youth and the middle generation, but also about those infants and children who either join them or are born in their adopted country; we are afraid all these are net loss

---

16 "Where Is Your Brother?", Appendix, sections 16.

for our country. As the saying goes, 'Getting used to has more impact than giving birth to'; and the children and grand-children of the ones who [we] have mentioned above will have the culture and identity of the places they were brought up in; and unless an effective campaign of instilling in them the love of their culture, country and people is waged; it will prove to be another problematic loss. But a country can only be built by those who stay inside to build it. Our country is hearing a cry of its depletion and bareness.[17]

5. As migration escalates, family cohesion not surprisingly is compromised. "Where Is Your Brother?" argues that the safety of a nation should not be seen in isolation from that of its families. The document states this deep truth by emphatically asserting that 'The family is the nucleus of the Church and the foundation of society'.

6. Under the subheading "Moral Building", the bishops discuss in detail the moral decay and corruption in their country. Although they do not provide a clear-cut answer on whether the corruption and decay is a consequence of societal failure or the result of the government's letdown, they argue that the lack of transparent administration and freedom of expression, as well as the spread of nepotism, paralysis, and destructive rumors, have created an enabling environment.

7. The document's main reproach strikes at the lack of rule of law. Various scholars, opposition groups, and concerned nationals have discussed this issue widely, especially outside the country. Nonetheless, three factors make "Where Is Your Brother?" particularly effective. i) Without external help, nationals living in the country, striving to bring about change from within, have produced the document. The bishops demonstrate their cognizance of this fact when they write, "A country can only be built by those who stay inside to build it". ii) The document clearly and bluntly points out the need to end unlawful arrests, begin respecting human rights, and implementing the constitution. iii) "Where Is Your Brother?" is the only such Church document that has been made public, despite the likelihood that other unpublicized documents have

---

17 Ibid., Appendix, section 18.

been criticizing the appalling situation. Regarding the supremacy of the rule of law, the bishops write:

> In the previous section, No. 12, we remembered that we have 'peaceful people who live in peace;' and it was right to see it as a blessing and good; but '…when we say peace, it does not only mean the absence of war; it is not a peace as a result of a balance of power among competing sides; it is not also a peace that comes due to a hegemonic or an all-powerful tyrannical system. When we say peace, we mean the 'enterprise of justice and fairness' (Isaiah 32) that is conducted through proper and right means.
>
> Peace falls in jeopardy when transgressions and injustices are let to blossom; and when jealousy, arrogance and mistrust reign supreme. The foundations of peace disappear when any man's rights and dignity are undermined, and is deprived of what is rightfully his. We don't say, 'justice delayed is justice denied' for nothing; but because it makes a strong foundation for peace, and it is for this why we need to expedite the dispensation of justice for those who are waiting for it, for those who are been (sic) sought by the law, and for those who are already in custody.[18]

8. Treating education as a key factor in the development and well-being of a nation, the pastoral letter calls for building and enhancing national educational institutions. In order for the national curriculum to be current and effective, it should avoid being purely academic and instead inculcate the concepts of "equality, democracy, justice, fairness, rule of law, and accountability". In the four bishops' view, education that creates social awareness spares a country from relying on external handouts and gradually puts it on a self-sustaining track.

It is true that before the Catholic bishops' critical intervention, other groups, scholars, and concerned nationals had indeed deliberated on many of the issues raised in "Where Is Your Brother?". Several of those who raised concerns focused on the need for constitutional governance, free press, and redress of various social justice issues. For example, in November 1992, in a seminar held in Asmara for writers

---

18   Ibid., Appendix, section 30.

and journalists, I spoke about the importance of freedom of speech and the dangers of censorship and self-censorship in a new nation. It is with deep sorrow that I revisit those remarks and quote the following few lines from the talk I delivered then under the title "The Freedom of the Writer":

> [A]ll this development about the emerging writings is only a sign of a promising renaissance, and one has to be careful not to be naïve and complacent in believing or thinking that, because there is no censorship at present or because the government is encouraging literature at present, our literature will henceforth blossom. Particularly, the writers will have to be alert against becoming victims of a paralyzing 'self-censorship' that expresses itself in thoughts such as 'we should not offend our government', or 'maybe our government will not like this', or 'if I write this, people will think this or that' ... [The reason] is because, once self-censorship becomes a norm in any country, it will certainly mutate itself gradually into government censorship.[19]

Other scholars and activists who had expressed concerns over Eritrea's growing lack of human rights and deteriorating conditions due to the war and repression include: Dan Connell in *Conversation with Eritrean Political Prisoners* (2004); Kidane Mengisteab and Okbazghi Yohannes, *Anatomy of An African Tragedy: Political, Economic and Foreign Policy Crisis in Post-Independence Eritrea* (2005); Gaim Kibreab in *Eritrea: A Dream Deferred* (2009); and websites such as www.awate.com, www.asmarino.com, www.assenna.com, and others. Also human right activists including Alganesh Ghandi, Father Mussie Zerai, Elsa Chyrum, Meron Estifanos, and Mirjam van Reisen have voiced concerns and criticism at different times. Moreover, we cannot fail to mention the former members of the government and national assembly known as the G-15, who disagreed with the state and have been arrested since 2001; and the diaspora-based Eritreans known as the G-13, who also disagreed with the government and joined the mainstream opposition.

The above examples of critical opposition are mentioned in order to argue that the recent pastoral letter was influenced by and is the culmination of gradually accumulating expressions of discontent. Yet,

---

19   Ghirmai Negash, "The Freedom of the Writer". Last accessed August 4, 2017. http://www.warscapes.com/retrospectives/eritrea/freedom-writer

it is important to take into account and understand the uniqueness of "Where Is Your Brother?" and to give it the special attention it deserves. Three factors make this pastoral letter unprecedented: 1) it's a document issued by religious leaders from inside the country (no other religious institution has openly expressed its objection to what is happening in Eritrea); 2) for taking a peaceful stand with the Eritrean people in opposition to the tyranny that they live under (sharing one's views with the public in an organized and peaceful manner is itself significant); and 3) more importantly from a theoretical perspective, for introducing the concept of liberation theology in Eritrea. As indicated in the introduction of this essay, the concept of liberation theology is new in the Eritrean context. Therefore, before launching into a discussion about the relevance of liberation theology in Eritrea and its advent in "Where Is Your Brother?", a brief discussion about the concept and its history is in order.

Liberation Theology in Latin America

Liberation theology was first conceived of in Latin American Catholic churches in the late 1960s at a "critical moment in modern Latin American history".[20] Rising against pervasive political repression, nepotism, poverty, and social injustices at all levels due to dictatorial regimes, the movement emerged in Argentina, Chile, Columbia, Peru, Guatemala, Nicaragua, and other places.[21] Historically, prior to the emergence of this movement, the Catholic Church had been tied with "conservatism" and "remained firmly allied with elites opposed to change in the established order of things generally".[22] Under the

---

20   Levine, "Assessing the Impacts of Liberation Theology in Latin America" (1988): 248. For earlier preliminary discussions on liberation theology in Europe, see Henri Gooren, "Catholic and Non-Catholic Theologies of Liberation: Poverty, Self-Improvement, and Ethics Among Small-Scale Entrepreneurs in Guatemala City," *Journal for the Scientific Study of Religion* 41, no. 1 (2002): 29.

21   Michael Dodson, "Liberation Theology and Christian Radicalism in Contemporary Latin America," *Journal of Latin American Studies* 11, no 1 (1979): 204; Henri Gooren, "Catholic and Non-Catholic Theologies of Liberation: Poverty, Self-Improvement, and Ethics among Small-Scale Entrepreneurs in Guatemala City," *Journal for the Scientific Study of Religion* 41, no 1 (2002): 30-31.

22   Levine, "Assessing the Impacts of Liberation Theology in Latin America" (1988): 241. See also Manzar Foroohar, "Liberation Theology: The Response of Latin American Catholics to Socioeconomic

influence of various social, political, and ideological movements – including Marxism[23] – and internal theological debates within the Church, however, some theologians and church leaders began to align themselves with the poor in their struggle for socio-political transformation and social justice. In countries where extreme dictatorships and excessive capitalist greed held sway, the Church's open embrace of a political stance on the side of the people constituted a watershed moment.[24]

Two distinct developments played a critical role in shaping the concept of Liberation Theology and its global reach. First was the 1971 publication of the Peruvian priest and theologian Gustavo Gutierrez's book, *A Theology of Liberation: History, Politics, and Salvation*.[25] Gutierrez's long experience of working among the poor of his country served as a basis for his book. The most crucial development setting the stage for the origin and consolidation of liberation theology was the 1968

Problems," *Latin American Perspectives* 13, no 3 (1986): 38, and Gooren, "Catholic and Non-Catholic Theologies of Liberation: Poverty, Self-Improvement, and Ethics among Small-Scale Entrepreneurs in Guatemala City" (2002): 31.

23   Dodson, "Liberation Theology and Christian Radicalism in Contemporary Latin America" (1979): 203; Gooren, "Catholic and Non-Catholic Theologies of Liberation: Poverty, Self-Improvement, and Ethics among Small-Scale Entrepreneurs in Guatemala City" (2002): 31.

24   Quoting Christian Smith, *The Emergence of Liberation Theology: Radical Religion and Social Movement Theory* (1991), Gooren in "Catholic and Non-Catholic Theologies of Liberation: Poverty, Self-Improvement, and Ethics among Small-Scale Entrepreneurs in Guatemala City," (2002): 30, writes:
[A] small cadre of young, aggressive, radicalized theologians outraged by Latin American poverty and dependency gained access to positions of influence in the Latin American Catholic Church. They did so at a critical time when, because of a growing organizational crisis and an increased ideological openness, the Church was searching for a new organizational strategy that would strengthen its ability to achieve its mission in society. The strategy of this cadre was to abandon alliance with Latin America's political, economic, and military elites, and establish ties instead with Latin America's poor masses. They wanted to redefine the church as an advocate of social justice, economic equality, human rights, anti-imperialism, and popular political participation.

25   Gustavo Gutierrez, *A Theology of Liberation: History, Politics, and Salvation* (Maryknoll, New York: Orbis Books, 1973). Originally published as *Teología de la liberación, Perspectivas* by CEP, Lima, 1971.

Second Conference of the Latin American Bishops in Medellin, Colombia.[26] Levine and Foroohar agree that the meeting constituted a landmark meeting that "set new dimensions for the Church's role in all aspects of regional life".[27]

The ideas of liberation theology have evolved over time to adapt to circumstances (including overcoming internal opposition from John Pope Paul II).[28] But its basic principles of solidarity with communities and groups of people who find themselves afflicted by poverty, oppression, and injustice are enduring, with its advocates remaining committed to "affirm that the basic questions of theology center [or should center] on poor people and the meaning of their experience".[29]

While concern with the poor remains the defining goal of liberation theology, scholars such as Barryman and Levine, who are interested in the scope and methods of liberation theology as a critical intellectual project, also state the importance of heeding attention to the historicity, intentionality, and upshot of the movement. In Levine's

---

26 Foroohar, "Liberation Theology: The Response of Latin American Catholics to Socioeconomic Problems," 40.

27 Levine, "Assessing the Impacts of Liberation Theology in Latin America" (1988): 248; Foroohar, "Liberation Theology: The Response of Latin American Catholics to Socioeconomic Problems," writes: "The Second Conference of Latin American Bishops at Medellin, Colombia, in 1968 was a culmination of this process of radicalization in the Latin American church." (1986): 40. She adds that, historically, "Traditional Catholicism views poverty as an individual failure and stresses charity and job training. In contrast, the bishops at Medellin meeting examined poverty in its social context and called for not only individual charity but a profound change in socioeconomic structure" (ibid.).

28 Gooren, in "Catholic and Non-Catholic Theologies of Liberation: Poverty, Self-Improvement, and Ethics among Small-Scale Entrepreneurs in Guatemala City," observes: "But the Catholic Church had changed significantly as well. In countries where liberation theology was traditionally strong, Pope John Paul II appointed more conservative new bishops and cardinals. The fact that liberation theology had originated and spread through enthusiastic leaders now became a weakness. The leaders were replaced or forbidden from expressing their views, such as the Brazilian Leonardo Boff and Nicaraguan Ernesto Cardenal" (2002): 31.

29 Levine, "Assessing the Impacts of Liberation Theology in Latin America" (1988): 245. See also Foroohar, "Liberation Theology: The Response of Latin American Catholics to Socioeconomic Problems" (1986).

words, "Liberation theology commits itself to listening to the poor and learning about the world as they see and experience it. Commitment and involvement with struggles for liberation are central, and therefore stances of dispassionate neutrality are dismissed as unrealistic and hypocritical".[30]

Given the long history of charity by the Catholic Church and its commitment to and support of the oppressed, what then makes Liberation Theology unique? As researchers in the field explain, its uniqueness lies in the fact that it improved on the old view of supporting the poor with charity to something more dynamic, transforming the lives of the poor from within.[31] Accordingly, it constitutes a departure from the general approach of giving help and moves toward examining and changing the structures and institutions that caused poverty in the first place. In other words, liberation theology explicitly views and examines society's political and economic issues through the lens of the poor, and in practice works and calls upon religious leaders and activist citizens to jointly advocate on behalf of the people.

Some commentators on liberation theology mistakenly view the movement's teachings on social justice as removed from the Catholic Church's main religious tenets. As those who study the movement contend, however, in the Latin American experience liberation theologians challenged and stood against violence and exploitation, positions firmly grounded in the spiritual teachings of the Catholic Church. In particular, using the Church's known prophets and angels as examples, they inspired the people to resist. In his book, *We Drink From Our Own Wells*, Gustavo Gutiérrez reaffirms the veracity of such a claim by stressing,

> The spirituality being born… is the spirituality of the church of the poor… the spirituality of an ecclesial community that is trying to make effective its solidarity with the poorest of the world. It is a

---

30 Levine, "Assessing the Impacts of Liberation Theology in Latin America" (1988): 246.

31 Philip Berryman in *Liberation Theology* (Philadelphia: Temple University Press, 1987) aptly captures the force and significance of liberation theology when he argues that "People do not simply happen to be poor; their poverty is largely a product of the way society is organized. Hence, liberation theology is a critique of economic structures that enable some Latin Americans to jet to Miami or London to shop, while most of their fellow citizens do not have safe drinking water" (5).

collective, ecclesial spirituality that, without losing anything of its universal perspective, is stamped with the religious outlook of an exploited and believing people… It is a new spirituality because the love of the Lord who urges us to reject inertia and inspires us to creativity is itself always new.[32]

Liberation Theology in Eritrea?

It would be fair to conclude that the document that the four Eritrean Catholic bishops released under the title "Where Is Your Brother?" reflects the fundamental principles of liberation theology as it played itself out in Latin America. Even though the two phenomena occurred in different times and places, their shared concern for the poor and rejection of exploitation and oppression link the struggles of the Latin American and Eritrean Churches. This does not mean that the Latin American manifestation of Liberation Theology necessarily drove its African counterpart in Eritrea, in light of the great geographical distance and limited direct linkages between the two.

As previously explained, "Where Is Your Brother?" strongly condemns the political and economic crises, lawlessness, and unbridled corruption resulting from a lack of leadership. If this document serves as a measure, the Eritrean Catholic Church clearly has chosen sides with the disenfranchised citizens of the country (the poor, the exiled, victims of accidents at sea and in the desert, and the imprisoned). Furthermore, the detailed descriptions of oppression, corruption, and other forms of injustice contained in page after page of the bishops' document carry all the more meaning because they, in accord with the document's aims, request a reform of the Eritrean political system. This courageous stand puts "Where Is Your Brother?" on the same plane as Latin American Liberation Theology.

Moreover, on close reading of the bishops' letter, one finds specific evidence of its analytical association with liberation theology. In this regard, the most salient features of the document are the passages where its authors trace their writing back to two theologically significant documents issued by the Roman Catholic Church to the followers of the faith. The first is a reference to one of Pope Francis's morning meditations – also titled "Where Is Your Brother?".[33] The

---

32 Quoted in Levine, "Assessing the Impacts of Liberation Theology in Latin America" (247).
33 Given in the Chapel of The *Domus Sanctae Marthae* under the title "Where Is Your Brother?", on Sunday, June 2, 2013. The Eritrean bishops write:

second is a direct quote from a pastoral letter by Pope Benedict XVI called "Crossing the Threshold of Faith".

It is not unusual for the Eritrean Catholic Church, as a widely spread religious institution, to issue statements about general moral deterioration and loss of religious direction, based on papal edicts. In this particular case, however, the bishops' references to the Vatican's specific teachings suggest that they wanted to communicate the papal blessing of what they were doing, as well as draw attention to the global dimension of their endeavor, in order to attract the world's eyes to Eritrea. In preparing their document, the Eritrean bishops used as a doctrinal basis Pope Benedict XVI's following call:

> The Church as a whole and all her Pastors, like Christ, must set out to lead people out of the desert, towards the place of life, towards friendship with the Son of God, towards the One who gives us life, and life in abundance. It often happens that Christians are more concerned for the social, cultural and political consequences of their commitment, continuing to think of the faith as a self-evident presupposition for life in society. In reality, not only can this presupposition no longer be taken for granted, but it is often openly denied. Whereas in the past it was possible to recognize a unitary cultural matrix, broadly accepted in its appeal to the content of the faith and the values inspired by it, today this no longer seems to be the case in large swathes of society, because of a profound crisis of faith that has affected many people.[34]

As previously stated, the Eritrean bishops' reference to Pope Francis' contemplation of June 2, 2013 bearing the same title, "Where Is Your Brother?", is the clearest demonstration of their intellectual debt to the Catholic Church. This connection is reinforced by the fact that before he became head of the Catholic Church, Pope Francis was an Argentinian priest who took part in the struggles of the people of that region. The Eritrean bishops' adaptation of "Where Is Your

---

"Pope Francis, in his last address asks us, "Where is your brother?" (Gn. 4:9). In order to look after the well-being of our brother, "which is helping us to sense the great joy of believing and to renew our wonder at the vast horizons which faith opens up, so as then to profess that faith in its unity and integrity, faithful to the memory of the Lord and sustained by his presence and by the working of the Holy Spirit" (Light of Faith by Pope Francis). See Appendix, section 4.

34 The Pope Emeritus, Benedict XVI, in his *Motu Proprio Porta Fidei*, 2, quoted in "Where is Your Brother?" (Section 3).

Brother?" directly from the sermon of Pope Francis evidences the relationship that exists – or ought to exist – between the Eritrean document and global liberation theology. A core issue, however, is whether what the Catholic bishops have begun in Eritrea heralds the advent of a sustaining liberation theology or an off-and-on phenomenon. Only time can provide answers.

Chapter Three

FROM THE MOUNTAINTOP TO THE EDGES OF THE PRECIPICE: AN AFRICAN POSTCOLONIAL STORY

Awet T. Weldemichael

With his examination and contextualization of "Where Is Your Brother?" in the previous chapter, Ghirmai Negash has challenged Eritreans to raise the bar of their consciousness, as well as the substance and method of their conversation about national politics in a global context. The ensuing chapter is a modest attempt to heed this call and follow his example by critically reflecting on how, in the first place, independent Eritrea reached the current state of equal opportunity oppression where none seem to escape Asmara's repressive apparatus. It does so by placing the Eritrean experience in the context of African decolonization: anticolonial revolutionary thought, armed struggles for liberation, and the postcolonial state.

In the heady run up to Ghana's independence, the country's founding president and preeminent Pan-Africanist Kwame Nkrumah famously bastardized a Biblical verse (Matthew 6:33 to be specific) declaring: "Seek ye first the political kingdom, and all else shall be added unto you."[1] African liberation movements mobilized their mostly illiterate constituencies by blaming their ills on colonialism and presenting as a panacea reclamation of the land – literally and

---

1   Quoted in Ali A. Mazrui, "Seek ye First the Political Kingdom," 105-126 [here 105] in Mazrui (ed.) *General History of Africa, Volume VIII: Africa Since 1935* (James Currey, University of California Press, and UNESCO 1999).

figuratively. Unfortunately, the pursuit of political independence without a footing in an independent economy left the postcolonial African state in deep crisis.[2] That crisis seems to be more serious in countries that sought and gained the political kingdom through armed struggle, delaying or derailing the hoped-for economic dividends of independence.

Whereas no expectations of independence have been satisfied quickly enough, nor will they ever be, "subjection" and "discipline", to use Cameroonian philosopher Achille Mbembe's rather pessimistic characterization, have become the norm in the African postcolony.[3] And, as stated, this was all the more so with countries that achieved decolonization after a protracted armed struggle – from Algeria to Mozambique and Guinea Bissau to Eritrea. As some of the direct combatants of the anticolonial wars ponder where they may have gone wrong, we find many citizens frustrated with sluggish or non-forthcoming dividends of independence, reminiscing – and some even waxing lyrical – about the dubious "good old days" of foreign colonial rule.

When Portuguese President Jorge Sampaio visited Mozambique in early 2005, in his final year as head of state, his host took him on a drive through the countryside and stopped to inspect a farm. With President Jaoquim Chisano on his side, President Sampaio introduced himself to a lone elderly peasant and asked him how he was doing. Without knowing with whom he was speaking, the Mozambican farmer reportedly complained about his lot and asked, "When is this independence thing going to be over? We were better off under the Portuguese."[4] Such revisionist romanticizing about the non-existent good old days reflects, more than anything, the disappointment of many Africans with the slow or unrealized promises of independence – especially where independence was only achieved after an arduous armed struggle that exacted a heavy toll on the people.

In a similar fashion to that of the Mozambican farmer, an Eritrean elder purportedly lamented the people's fate after independence to one

---

2   Almost five decades after Nkrumah, in 1992 U.S. election campaign strategist (of then Governor Clinton's presidential bid) James Carville mumbled "the economy, stupid," which became a viral campaign slogan and curt rebuttal to political talk devoid of economic considerations.

3   Achille Mbembe, *On the Postcolony* (Berkeley: University of California Press, 2001), 102ff.

4   Confidential conversations with a member of President Jorge Sampaio's entourage (Summer 2006, Lisbon, Portugal).

of the senior leaders of Eritrea's liberation movements: "Having lived under Italian, British, federal, and Ethiopian administrations, let me tell you, my son, that your administration is incompetent, your manners uncouth, and your currency worthless. It is a cruel irony that we are worse off today under the rule of our own children."[5] Some have cited the daunting challenges that these countries faced – and some continue to face – after independence to conclude how wrong it was for them to seek independence in the first place. Some Eritreans are openly advocating for a resurrection of the externally imposed and ultimately failed association with Ethiopia, whereas others seem to have, at least on one occasion, openly expressed the wish to merge with Sudan.[6] Meanwhile, many are actively pursuing narrowly defined identity politics and sowing the seeds of hateful intolerance, and many more seem to be wallowing in self-hate.

However unfortunate, government failings in the post-independence era do not render colonialism any less degrading, dehumanizing, and exploitative. Nonetheless, it remains important to ask and seek answers for why so many seemingly righteous movements with decisive popular support turned out to be such colossal failures after independence.[7] In offering preliminary answers to this question, I examine the dichotomous landscape where violent practices of the liberation movements often clashed with the aspired post-independence regime of citizen rights and opportunities.

To begin with, the structurally violent world order so far has hamstrung the culmination of the democratic origins and liberatory aspirations of African anti-colonial struggles. The international state

---

5   Andebrhan Welde Giorgis, *Eritrea at a Crossroads: A Narrative of Triumph, Betrayal and Hope* (Houston: Strategic Book Publishing and Rights Co., 2014), 618 (epigraph).

6   However few they may be in number, these are mostly Europe-based Eritreans (and mostly in the UK), with the Christian highlanders warming up to Ethiopia, and Muslim lowlanders suggesting to Sudanese politicians their considerations to join Sudan instead.

7   Lest we apply a broad Afro-pessimist brush across the continent (and throughout its post-independence decades), it is important to acknowledge that Africa has, since independence, made and continues to make admirable gains in spite of the many ongoing foreign and domestic challenges. Mildly put, the point here is that, in countries that had to resort to protracted armed struggle for independence, the gains far belie the sacrifices that the concerned peoples endured, and the support that they lent their movements and the early governments that followed them.

system is rigged against the weak, newly independent former colonies on the continent. The very constellation of regional and global forces and interests that prompted African nationalists to resort to armed struggle in the first place contributed significantly to the delay or derailment of a central goal of decolonization, the consummation of liberation. The newly independent countries could not deliver on the promises of independence because they either caved in to realpolitik and submitted to greater power interests, or they were cast away for refusing to do so, often in collusion with their neighboring or far-away former colonizers.[8] Within such a violent structural framework, the means by which independence was achieved did not guarantee the post-independence freedoms necessary for the anticipated socioeconomic and political dividends. Indeed, those violent means often subverted the prospects for desired freedoms to be achieved.

Compelled by the violent regional and global structures to resort to armed struggle, African nationalists had to match the militaristic dispositions of their oppressors. In the process, and especially after decolonization, many of them grew increasingly indistinguishable from the environment out of which they arose and against which they struggled. The enveloping life-or-death conditions made them regard their own people as either against them or with them: the former to be vanquished; the latter to be mobilized, organized, and placed under a strict regime of discipline in order to bolster the struggle. The mechanics of enforcing such a regime of discipline proved detrimental to the much anticipated, truly liberated, democratic polity. After prolonged violent struggle for independence, these post-colonies themselves often used force in its crudest forms. They relied on the same oppressive and violent methods that had ensured liberation from colonial rule to the detriment of nurturing a truly liberated society.

Although the independence movements were not monolithic wholes, the military component that prevailed operationally failed to see the distinction between liberation and mere decolonization. Besides the objective eviction of the colonizer and resulting control of territory, however, liberation ought to consist of important prerequisites that are as subjective as they are objective, i.e. political freedom, social justice, and an overall regime of human security

---

8   Africans and non-Africans alike have produced a rich literature on this issue. For the most recent and accessible account, see Elizabeth Schmidt, *Foreign Intervention in Africa: From the Cold War to the War on Terror* (Cambridge: Cambridge University Press, 2013).

guarantees. Unfortunately, although advocates for rights and freedoms during and after the victorious struggles strived for something more substantial, democratic and humane than mere decolonization, these lofty ideals and goals often did not transfer over to fighters and grass-roots supporters, beyond their situational utility in the context of the raging wars against the colonizers. The circumstances of war and the lack of sustained debate about or experience with the practicalities of liberation shrank the democratic spaces and nurtured militarism instead.

An intrinsic contradiction between the ideal of liberation and the means of the movements that resorted to armed struggle thus blighted the process of liberation and plagued the newly independent countries. Alexis de Tocqueville perhaps best captured – in political terms – how the fruit does not fall far from the tree. In his classic work on the French and American Revolutions, de Tocqueville posited that the revolutionaries were not and could not have been better than the environment from which and against which they arose. Because, he was "convinced that... they took from the old régime not only most of its customs, conventions, and modes of thought, but even those very ideas which prompted our revolutionaries to destroy it; that in fact, *though nothing was further from their intentions, they used the debris of the old order for building up the new*" (emphasis added).[9]

Similarly, when confronted with the inevitable domestic and foreign pressures of governance, the African anticolonial revolutionaries had few role models other than the repressive exercise of authority by the erstwhile colonial state and their own tested repertoire of power. This became particularly salient and grotesque when, immediately after independence, African nationalists succumbed to the near-universal dictates of politics, i.e. the urge to hold on to power in order to implement (genuine or not) one or another vision that they espoused. The successful habits and practices cultivated during long arduous years of struggle do not die easily. From Algeria, Guinea Bissau and Angola to Mozambique and Eritrea, those practices took a life of their own and ultimately became the rule.

Yet, asking whether African liberation movements compromised themselves and their noble cause by resorting to violence places the oppressed on the same plane as the oppressor, unduly legitimizing the latter. This is because colonial and secondary colonial powers' refusal

---

9   Alexis de Tocqueville, *The Old Régime and the French Revolution*, Trans. Stuart Gilbert (New York: Anchor Books, 1983), vii.

to peacefully grant independence left African nationalists with no choice but to take up arms. Nevertheless, one cannot escape the basic question of how these newly liberated countries foundered, especially in light of their moral high ground and political and military victories. Without passing judgment on African nationalists' resort to violence or privileging pacifism, my suggestions depart from an idealized fascination with violence and challenge the Fanonian concept of nationalist/revolutionary violence as a liberating act in and of itself.

Frantz Fanon and African Anticolonial Violence

I will briefly revisit Frantz Fanon, as an articulate theorist and proponent of violent struggle against colonialism, in order to show the disparity between his predictions/vision and developments on the ground where armed liberation movements won independence. Doing so will enable the juxtaposing – if only in passing – of the thought processes of yesteryear with the normative paradigms of the contemporary era. As in his early thinking about blackness, as well as his understanding of the particulars of anticolonial violence, Fanon was influenced by his former teacher, the black thinker Aimé Césaire. It is very likely that Fanon purposefully improvised the latter's graphic artistry of the slave's resort to violence in pursuit of freedom, and adapted it to decolonization. He particularly refers to *Et les chiens se taisaient* ("And the Dogs Were Silent"):

> My family name: offended; my given name: humiliated; my profession: rebel; my age: the stone age"
> …it is not you [mother/lover] who will prepare it [freedom] with your disarmament;
> it is *I* with my revolt and my poor clenched fists and bushy head.[10]

Fanon – like Che Guevara[11] – rightly believed that when colonialism prevailed in violation of preexisting laws and practices, and persisted against the wishes of the colonized, it handed the latter the right to resist in any way they saw fit. Fanon did not champion violence for its own sake, nor was he oblivious to the corrosive effects of

---

10 Frantz Fanon, *The Wretched of the Earth*, Trans. Richard Philcox (New York: Grove Press, 2004), 44.

11 "When the forces of oppression come to maintain themselves in power against established law, peace is considered already broken." Ernesto "Che" Guevara, *Guerrilla Warfare*, Third Edition (Lanham: Scholarly Resources Inc., 1997), 51.

violence on society.[12] He, nonetheless, believed that the colonized could restore their courage, dignity, and humanity through the same violence that the colonizer used to humiliate and dehumanize the colonized. Accordingly, the violent counter-measures of the colonized become "totalizing since each [colonized] individual represents a violent link in the great chain, the almighty body of violence,"[13] in which and through which the "colonized man liberates himself."[14] Violence, in Fanonian parlance, cleanses the colonized of their "inferiority complex, of their passive and despairing attitude."[15] Thus emboldened and with their self-confidence restored, they "realize that liberation was the achievement of each and every one and no special merit should go to the leader."[16] That realization supposedly explains what Fanon perceived to be the "aggressive tendency [of the colonized] to distrust the system of protocol that young governments are quick to establish. When they have used violence to achieve national liberation, the masses allow nobody to come forward as 'liberator'. Totally irresponsible yesterday, today they are bent on understanding everything and determining everything."[17]

Fanon's analytical preoccupation with the use of force against the external enemy in a colonial and/or neocolonial setting prevented him from treating violence as a double-edged sword. Even when he spoke of how the "apotheosis of independence becomes the curse of independence,"[18] he was referring to the external element about which the people are sufficiently enlightened to jealously protect their gains. While he was right that circumstances left violence as a final recourse for the colonized, the few decades of African independence mostly have confirmed Fanonian theorizing on violence as overly optimistic

---

12   In the chapter on "Colonial War and Mental Disorders," Fanon documents a few psychiatric cases that he treated. "Case No. 5" presents a French colonial police inspector whose job involved torturing Algerian freedom fighters of the FLN and their suspected sympathizers. The colonial officer started to beat his children and wife, and fantasized about beating up anyone who stood on his way. He sought professional help in order to stop torturing his family and control his tempers without stopping his work. Fanon, *The Wretched of the Earth*, 196-199.

13   Fanon, *The Wretched of the Earth*, 50.

14   Ibid., 44.

15   Fanon, *The Wretched of the Earth*, 51.

16   Ibid.

17   Ibid., 51-52.

18   Ibid., 54.

and utopian at best. They have accordingly been critiqued from different angles, most famously by Hanna Arendt, and most recently by Aaronette White.[19]

Fanon's astute observations of the crises that gripped the newly independent countries and those that were still fighting colonialism at that time rested on class analysis of the various sectors of the independent body politic and their respective failings. Those include behavioral and materialistic deficiencies of the leaders, their overall ineptitude, and the conspicuous absence of a middle class.[20] The contradiction between the violent means and processes of liberation, on the one hand, and the ideal of liberation, on the other, is not accounted for in Fanonian or any other nationalist discourse on the virtues of violence against colonialism. Nor are the consequent and unavoidable weeds of armed liberation struggle: the demons within and among the liberators and the systematically inculcated habits of obedience among the people that necessarily played a role in the struggle for liberation.

Deteriorating conditions on the ground and a related normative shift threw Fanon's aforementioned analyses off the mark. The erosion of – or delay in restoring – the rights of the newly liberated citizens amid spiraling violence that those countries experienced at the turn of the century are particularly poignant. Such tragedies and challenges of independence contributed to a decided discursive shift toward a "Responsibility to Protect".[21] It thus becomes important to examine

---

19 Hanna Arendt, *On Violence* (San Diego: Harcourt Brace & Company, 1970); Aaronette M. White, "All the Men Are Fighting for Freedom, All the Women Are Mourning Their Men, but Some of Us Carried Guns: A Raced-Gendered Analysis of Fanon's Psychological Perspectives on War," *Signs*, Vol. 32, No. 4 (Summer 2007), pp. 857-884.

Arendt is careful to add that she uses Fanon because of his influence on the 1960s student generation but that Fanon himself was "much more doubtful about violence than his admirers." Arendt, *On Violence*, 14, fn. 19. Preeminent African scholar Mahmood Mamdani, by contrast, has a favorable take on Fanon's prescience. See Mamdani, *When Victims Become Killers: Colonialism, Nativism, and the Genocide in Rwanda* (Princeton and Oxford: Princeton University Press, 2001), 10 and 13.

20 Ibid., 97ff.

21 International Commission on Intervention and State Sovereignty (ICISS), *Responsibility to Protect* (Ottawa: the International Development Research Centre 2001). Last accessed August 1, 2017: http://responsibilitytoprotect.org/ICISS% 20Report.pdf.

how the resort to violence in pursuit of liberation carried a structural flaw that, when not wisely managed, threatened the very cause of liberation and also became a serious impediment to the long-term stability of the newly independent countries. Before critiquing the shortcomings of their processes and outcomes, however, one should recognize the rightful place of African liberation struggles as pioneering proponents and agents of the liberation paradigm, at the time when many of the current advocates of the "R2P" idea were in fact deniers of African fundamental rights.

One of the most essential goals of African liberation was to free nationals from the exploitative and humiliating colonial subjugation. In that sense alone, African pursuit of decolonization was just and legal in nature. Building on the United Nations Charter and the Universal Declaration of Human Rights, U.N. General Assembly Resolutions 1514 and 1541 of December 1960 famously made denying the right of self-determination to a people tantamount to a violation of their fundamental human rights. Independence from colonialism – whether European or African colonialism of a bigger neighbor or a white minority government stepping into the shoes of the erstwhile colonial power – thus becomes inherently democratic as well. But the growth of these initial liberationist and democratic manifestations was and continues to be held back, first, by the means through which independence was sought and achieved, and second, by the lack of sustained debate about, awareness of, and experience with the practicalities of liberation.

Once they took to violence as a last resort, African nationalists could not afford to risk the consequences of being less militaristic than their oppressors. Alas, this made it more difficult to lay the foundations of a truly liberated, democratic polity afterwards. Militarism demanded and entrenched authoritarian control, bred rigid top-down hierarchies, dismissed many liberties as unaffordable luxuries, and instilled acceptance of the suspension of some fundamental rights for the greater good of the cause – the achievement of national independence.[22] The *modus operandi* of armed revolutionary movements was that the foe would be defeated and the ally brought into its fold in various ways to bolster the struggle. Once brought into the nationalist movement, the civilian population – like the active combatants –

---

22   Alex de Waal (ed.), *Demilitarizing the Mind: African Agendas for Peace and Security* (Trenton, NJ and Asmara: Africa World Press, 2002), 73ff.

became subject to a strict regime of discipline necessitated by the circumstances of war.

After colonial troops departed or were vanquished, those in positions of power in the postcolonial African state proved unable and unwilling to allow democratization. As a result of a corrosive mix of persistent militarism, power's demonstrated inability to democratize itself, and the unwillingness of those in power to relinquish that power, the state in such post-colonies exercised authority in its crudest forms. When confronted with inherently messy pressures of governance, the African anticolonial revolutionaries had little to fall back on save the time-tested repertoire of power as exercised during the decolonization process. This became particularly salient and grotesque when, immediately after independence, African nationalists succumbed to the near-universal dictates of politics, i.e. the urge to cling to power in order to implement (genuinely or not) one or another vision or agenda that they espoused. Sadly, Eritrea is no exception to such unintended consequences of violence ensuing from armed independence struggles.

From a Revolutionary Vision to a Nightmarish Reality in Eritrea

The Eritrean nationalist cause envisioned a pluralistic, democratic society where the rights and freedoms of the people would be protected and the values of the society upheld. This was initially postulated by the Eritrean Liberation Movement (ELM, or Harakat al-Tahrir al-Irytria in its Arabic name), subsequently espoused by the armed Eritrean Liberation Front (ELF) and ultimately carried to triumphant military conclusion by the Eritrean People's Liberation Front (EPLF). Following the 1991 military victory and the successful self-determination referendum in 1993, these aspirations were broadly articulated in what otherwise would have been foundational documents of the post-independence political dispensation.[23] They, unfortunately, remain unimplemented and the Eritrean public disempowered for a number of reasons, starting from the leadership and structures of the nationalist movement and the independent government that it ushered.

To many Eritreans, including some of his old and recent opponents, the current president of Eritrea, Isaias Afwerki, personified the vision for independent Eritrea and the brilliant strategy that turned that vision into reality. Indeed, at numerous critical moments in the

---

23   Andebrhan Welde Giorgis, *Eritrea at a Crossroads*, 155ff.

arduous armed struggle, he proved his mettle and earned the admiration of many and the respect and/or the fear of the rest. He inspired staunch loyalty among his lieutenants, whom he carefully identified and kept close – notably, in a well-contained maze of creative tensions between them. He was known to be very studious and thorough during the struggle years. His meticulous preparation of and for the agenda of every meeting of the Politburo of the Eritrean People's Liberation Front (EPLF) and his attention to detail helped him to easily surmount any opposition he faced – and he faced a lot – by addressing them in his own terms. Over time, his colleagues came to increasingly trust and rely on him for thoroughness, foresight, decision, and even arbitration among them, sowing the seeds of future discord.

Asked to identify the secret behind the spectacular successes of the EPLF (and its equally spectacular failures after independence), Ambassador Andebrhan Welde Giorgis attributed it to "strategic command and operational autonomy!".[24] Between the strategic vision and centralized control of the top leadership of the EPLF thus spearheaded by Isaias Afwerki on the one hand, and the subordinate cadres' tactical autonomy and operational command and finesse on the other, the second half of the Eritrean independence struggle made steady headway until independence. Nevertheless, problems emerged for the newly independent country when the two tiers of leaders began drifting apart from each other. The suddenly deepening rift between them also led to a chasm between both of them, on the one hand, and the Eritrean people in general, on the other. The once engaged, conscious, empowered public that had carried the independence movement to victory by hiding and nursing its wounded, providing supplies and intelligence, and most importantly, replenishing its fighting forces, found itself without the space and mechanisms to remain engaged. The people gradually lost ownership of the national project. With fraying popular support and without effective operatives and middle-ranking cadres, the vision for independent Eritrea slowly turned into an unending nightmare for its people.

A secret party had run the EPLF from behind the scenes and proved instrumental in helping make the movement's successes possible. Established in the early 1970s, the clandestine Eritrean People's Revolutionary Party (later Socialist Party) controlled the

---

24 Conversations with Ambassador Andebrhan Welde Giorgis, November 2015.

EPLF from the top all the way down to the smallest military and non-military units. Unknown to the non-members, the party maintained a secret chain through which information passed from below and command from above. It also instilled in its fighters (and through them among its civilian support base) the sense of unquestioning sacrifice and religious obedience to superiors. Nevertheless, holding one another accountable only occurred through a horizontal process of criticism and self-criticism that fell far short from a system of checks and balances.[25] As a result, the very mechanism of success during the armed struggle in Eritrea harbored the roots of the current abysmal failures.

During the secret congress that laid the groundwork for the 1987 Second and Unity Congress of the EPLF, the clandestine party concluded that victory against the withering Ethiopian military was inevitable. In preparation for the heightened military, political, and diplomatic coordination required for the birthing of a nation, all the structures of resistance and authority were further centralized around the newly elected secretary general of the EPLF, who also retained his leadership of the secret party. Once the powers of what upon independence became the executive branch of government were sufficiently centralized, discussions reportedly began about the redundancy of the secret party.[26] It was effectively suspended on order of its secretary general, Isaias Afwerki, until its official disbanding during the 1994 congress.[27] Meanwhile, the sprouts of a functioning democratic society that had mushroomed during the days of struggle – labor unions, professional associations, and gender- or age-based organizations – were "either dormant or reduced to service providers" after independence.[28]

---

25 Although the full story of the EPLF's secret party remains to be written, a few scholarly and popular publications and interviews shed light on its operations. See Dan Connell, "Inside the EPLF: The Origins of the 'People's Party' and its Role in the Liberation of Eritrea," *Review of African Political Economy* 28, no 89 (2001): 345-364; Col. Tsegu Fessahaie Bahta, *Eta Hebieti Selfi (The Hidden Party)* (Negarit Media, 2014).

26 Dan Connell, *Conversations with Eritrean Political Prisoners* (Trenton, NJ: Red Sea Press, 2005), 81-82.

27 Awet Tewelde Weldemichael, *Third World Colonialism and Strategies of Liberation: Eritrea and East Timor Compared* (New York: Cambridge University Press, 2013), 261, 291.

28 Connell, "Eritrea: Enough! A Critique of Eritrea's Post-Liberation Politics," a paper presented at the annual African Studies Association

Envisioned as organic tools of the struggle within the Eritrean nationalists' emerging grand strategy of broadening the arenas of resistance, the youth, student, women, farmer and worker associations emerged as structural extensions of the nationalist, anti-colonial movement. These mass organizations were directly administered by, or received directives from, the nationalist leadership, which also had mechanism to ensure they served their prescribed purposes. During the heightened military operations following the 1987 congress, all the mass organizations were dismantled under the guise of mobilizing all able-bodied nationals for the final phase of the intensifying war of liberation. Leaders and members of these organizations closed shop around 1988 and entered the field in various military, political, and administrative capacities under direct command of the field leadership.

After independence, the former mass organizations and village assemblies were not permitted to resume as vehicles – however controlled – of continued citizen engagement with the fledgling state. In 1993, the government shut down the Regional Centre for Human Rights and Development, the only independent, home-grown civil society organization to emerge after Eritrea's liberation, a mere two years into its existence. These measures effectively disempowered the civilian population, sparing the nascent government the nuisance of a conscious, organized public that was easy to mobilize.

Having witnessed the accomplishments of mass organizations and popular assemblies in Eritrea since the 1970s, Dan Connell expressed surprise at seeing them frozen after independence. Raising his concerns (like many others) about the negative repercussions of these moves at the time, he claims to: 1) have been "swayed by those who insisted they would revive the bottom-up popular movement once the institutional framework for the new state was in place"; 2) have been won over by the argument that a private local NGO gaining ample attention and outside support was "not the time for such an initiative when the front's mass organizations were struggling to establish themselves as self-financing, autonomous social movements"; 3) have found solace in the "uniquely participatory constitution-making process that drew in most of the Eritrean population at home and abroad from 1995 into 1997"; and 4) have observed "on the positive side… the evidence everywhere of the continuing commitment to

conference (Washington, DC, November 2003) and published by allAfrica.com. Also available at: http://www.danconnell.net/sites/default/files/Enough-A%20critique.pdf

egalitarian social and economic development – the new schools, the training centers for women, the village health stations, the new rural roads, and much more."[29]

He came to full grips with the political dangers of those moves two decades later when he reflected:

> An alarm I could no longer ignore sounded... when I learned that the popularly elected village assemblies – a hallmark of the movement since the 1970s – had been replaced by a system of party appointees who presided over village forums that no longer had political power of their own... Village self-government was where the people learned how to express themselves, identify their interests, make decisions, choose and hold accountable their leaders... This was the country's school for democracy, where the mechanisms of popular governance would be developed and tested and out of which a genuinely democratic national culture could grow. Told that these assemblies were not functioning "efficiently" enough, I nearly gagged. The argument that the people are not suited to govern themselves is as old as Plato. And what it leads to – rule from the top, whether by one man or a few, in the name of the people or not – is well documented.[30]

Meanwhile, public pronouncements and programmatic documents setting democratic ideals as cornerstones of an open society contributed to allaying some concerns. During the early 1994 congress when it converted itself into the ruling People's Front for Democracy and Justice (PFDJ), the independence movement encapsulated the aspirations that nationalists had pursued for the preceding three bloody decades. Its duly promulgated national charter stated:

> Our vision is for Eritrea to become a country where peace, justice, democracy and prosperity prevail. Our vision is to eliminate hunger, poverty and illiteracy from Eritrea. Our vision is for Eritrea to preserve its identity and uniqueness, develop commitment to family and community care, and by advancing economically, educationally and technologically, find itself among the developed countries. Our vision is for Eritrean society to be known for harmony among its different sectors, gender equality, love of country, humanity, discipline, hard work and love for knowledge, respect for law and

---

29   Ibid.
30   Ibid.

order, independence and inventiveness. Our vision is to perform miracles in peaceful nation-building as we did in the war of liberation.[31]

Of the "six basic goals" that summarize PFDJ's vision, the second deals with "political democracy" and reads: "For the people of Eritrea, to be active participants and become decision-makers in the administration and conduct of their lives and of their country, with their rights guaranteed by law and in practice."[32] Unfortunately, the lived experiences of ordinary Eritreans during the two decades that have since lapsed could not have been further from these admirable aspirations and goals.

The aftermath of the 1998-2000 war with Ethiopia brought to the fore the latent contradictions that Connell and others had noted with alarm in the early 1990s. The promised dividends of independence as well as the above assurances and encouraging signs remain unconsummated. With the middle- and high-ranking officials of the independence movement-cum-government groomed to take orders and the public systematically disempowered, the mechanics of democratic practices have yet to be internalized, making Eritrea one more postcolonial African state in crisis – the calm in the streets notwithstanding. Less than a decade since independence, the myopic logic of survival seemed to have overtaken the vision and strategy that once rallied a diverse and geographically scattered population, and that took friend and foe by storm. This predicament was not inevitable, however.

Lukewarm Citizenship Forfeiting Civic Vision

The leaders of independent Eritrea had selflessly offered themselves as sacrificial lambs for their people's liberation. Their becoming prisoners of the method through which they liberated their people, coupled with their staunch conviction on the continued righteousness of their intentions, has brought about one of the worst forms of domestic oppression. It is analogous to C.S. Lewis's astute observation, which he made in relation to capital punishment in his own country: "Of all tyrannies, a tyranny sincerely exercised for the good of its victims may be the most oppressive. [Because the]...

---

31 *National Charter for Eritrea* (approved by the Third Congress of the Eritrean People's Liberation Front, EPLF, Nacfa, February 1994), 10.
32 Ibid., 10-11.

omnipotent moral busybodies... who torment us for our own good will torment us without end for they do so with the approval of their own conscience."[33] The Eritrean Catholic bishops' pastoral letter, "Where Is Your Brother?", is one of several solemn chronicles of the consequences that occurred in spite of stern warnings by Eritrea's own visionaries.

That independent Eritrea continues to stagger on the edges of the precipice is an epic tragedy in the personal and collective histories and legacies of those who shepherded the country to independence, as well as to the future of the people they fought so hard to liberate. This profoundly sad turn of events was not inevitable, especially in light of the existence of alternative visions. Eritrea had no shortage of visionary civic leaders before and after independence who advised humility, inclusion, and reconciliation, leaders who alternatively cautioned sternly against hubris, exclusion, and predation.

Over a period of five decades, one of Eritrea's pioneer patriots, Woldeab Woldemariam, for example, wrote and spoke about the whole gamut of potential pitfalls and rewards flowing from how a people conducted themselves. In January 1944, he editorialized about the meaning of *hagher*, i.e. country, and the love of one's country. He wrote that the people constituted a country, not its physical features. Accordingly, the love of one's people constituted one's love for his/her country, and is rooted in "the fear of God... love of one's family and love of one's comrade."[34] More than four decades later, he met EPLF leaders (the present leaders of Eritrea) and Eritrean cultural icons on the sidelines of the Eritrean Bologna Festival in August 1987. Directly addressing the artists, he pointed out the significance of their craft in national reawakening. The parable he related of the three men (a swimmer, a warrior, and a musician) who rescued a princess from a beast in the deep sea can be said to be a metaphoric address equally to the political leaders that they constituted no more than one part of what the country had – and will need.[35]

---

33 C. S. Lewis, *God in the Dock: Essays on Theology and Ethics*, ed. Walter Hooper (Grand Rapids, Michigan: William B. Eerdmans Publishing Company, 2014), Chapter 4: "The Humanitarian Theory of Punishment," 318-333 [here 324].

34 Woldeab Woldemariam, "Hagher," in *Semunawi Gazzeta*, No. 75, 31 January 1944 reproduced in *Murutsat 'Anqetsat Ato Weldeab, 1941-1991*, Ed. Tikabo Aresei (Asmara, Eritrea: Hidri Publishers, 1995), 1-2.

35 According to the parable, because the beast liked music, the musician played music to get him out of the water and keep him distracted; the

The huge task of liberating a people and rebuilding a country required the collective effort of all members of the society just as the three men played their respective roles to rescue the princess. For the same reason that none of the three men could marry the princess as reward for saving her, no individual or group could be entitled to single handedly own the country. The prescient Woldeab was warning against exclusion rationalized by a sense of entitlement derived from one's service to the country. He had long endorsed instead a strong, inclusive national fabric rooted in the love of fellow citizens as one would love one's own family.

Immediately after liberation from Ethiopian rule, the call for intra-Eritrean dialogue, reconciliation, and inclusion reverberated across the country. Within a week of military victory, the Eritrean Liberation Front – Revolutionary Council (ELF-RC), one of several of ELF splinters after the latter was pushed out of the field in 1981, issued a statement in which it recognized EPLF's proclamation of the Provisional Government of Eritrea, committed itself to the preservation and enhancement of the achievement of victory, and called, among other things, for "an agreement/harmony that involves all national political forces in order to ensure national independence and equanimity."[36] While expressing confidence in the political leaders and exuding the inescapable euphoria of the time, the Eritrean Catholic Church became, in July 1991, the first non-political entity to similarly call for reconciliation and unity while celebrating diversity of individuals as well as groups.[37]

Around the same time, several Eritreans from within and outside the EPLF ranks called for an inclusive process of reconciling old differences and jointly charting out the future of the country in

---

warrior struck out the eyes of the beast and blinded him; and the swimmer then swam across the water and fetched the princess.

36 RDC/Hist/ELF, 02927, **"ተጋድሎ ሓርነት ኤርትራ - ስውራዊ ባይቶ፤ አጋዳሲ. መግለጺ.፤"** 30 May 1991. Eritrean Liberation Front – Revolutionary Council, "Important Announcement," 30 May 1991 (a document available at the Research and Documentation Center in Asmara, Eritrea).

37 **"ሰላምን ምዕብልናን፤ ብዝተሓደስ መንፈስ ንሓዳስ ኤርትራ። ሓዋርያዊ መልእኽቲ ንምእመናንን ንኹሎም ሰብ ጽቡቕ ድላይን"** ሓምለ 1991 ዓ.ም.ፈ. in **ካቶሊካውያን ጳጳሳት ኤርትራ፤ መንፈድታቱ አቓኖ፦ ሓዋርያዊ መልእኽታትን ሰነዳትን (1991– 2007)** (Bologna: Editrice Missionaria Italiana, 2008), 34.

accordance with basic principles of democracy and human rights. Prominent among these were Paulos Tesfagiorgis, who had directed the EPLF-affiliated Eritrean Relief Association (ERA) since its inception in the mid-1970s, and Dr. Taha Mohamed Nur. Since co-founding the Eritrean Liberation Front (ELF) in Cairo in 1960 and throughout the 30-year struggle, Taha Mohamed Nur worked for independence in various capacities, including as a member of the ELF Supreme Council. Since the mid-1970s, he had been a ranking leader of the ELF-PLF under Osman Saleh Sabbe. Upon independence, he publicly withdrew from his organization (then led by Omar Buruj) and voluntarily returned to Eritrea for, in his own words, he "was struggling for freedom and Eritrea was free."[38] Upon returning to Eritrea, he wrote a letter to the Eritrean leader, future President Isaias Afwerki (and brought it up during their subsequent meeting) about the need for a national conference to heal the wounds of the fractious and fratricidal past and bring all Eritreans on board with a common national agenda.

Given that power as a rule does not make concessions unless compelled to, such visionary pointers needed proactive citizenship in order to turn into reality. In an August 1857 address on "West India Emancipation," the African-American abolitionist orator Frederick Douglass timelessly captured the perils of an apathetic, submissive or trusting citizenry: "Power concedes nothing without a demand. It never did and it never will. Find out just what any people will quietly submit to and you have found out the exact measure of injustice and wrong which will be imposed upon them, and these will continue till they are resisted...".[39] The level of repression in Eritrea is not only a poignant measure of the endurance of the oppressed but, as Douglass pointed out, also of the citizens' active or passive complicity so subtly expressed in "Where is Your Brother?".

Any people get the government that they deserve and not one that they necessarily wish for. While cognizant of extenuating circumstances and especially the devastating 1998-2000 border conflict with Ethiopia, the vast majority of Eritreans have played varying levels

---

38 Conversations with Dr. Taha Mohamed Nur, September 2005.

39 Frederick Douglass, "If There Is No Struggle, There Is No Progress" (On August 3, 1857, Frederick Douglass delivered a "West India Emancipation" speech at Canandaigua, New York. See more at: http://www.blackpast.org/1857-frederick-douglass-if-there-no-struggle-there-no-progress#sthash.IIyScRxi.dpuf).

of active or passive roles in – and bear ordered or hierarchical responsibility for – what has become of independent Eritrea. Whereas some may have worked actively for the system and others contributed (directly or indirectly) to enable it, the vast majority either did not care enough or were too trusting of the system when core principles of good citizenship required them to be vigilant at all times. In this regard, a good deal of the failure could be ascribed to those Eritreans who had come of age long before independence – especially educated Eritreans.

From early on, the country's educated elite played the all-important role of articulating Eritrean aspirations and representing their collective interests – sometimes in contravention of the express instructions of religious (Christian and Muslim) leaders aligned with or controlled by the Ethiopian monarch. From Woldeab Woldemariam, Ibrahim Sultan, Abdulkadir Kebire and others in the 1940s, to the leaders of the Eritrean Liberation Movement (ELM) in 1958 and the founders of the ELF in 1960, Eritreans followed their highest educated members in grappling with their circumstances and taking ownership of their affairs. The influence of Eritrean intellectuals during the war of independence is discernible in every major transformative development of the nationalist movement. From 1964 onwards, the injection of large numbers of progressively more educated fighters into the ranks of the ELF first, and then of both ELF and EPLF, brought about all of the major organizational, military, political, humanitarian, and diplomatic milestones of the armed struggle.[40]

At independence and during the following formative years (between 1991 and 1997), Eritrea was blessed with citizens of the highest caliber, with remarkable education, vast political-academic-intellectual and other experiences, and of great international renown – all of whom played active roles in the country's sociopolitical and economic revival. This gave Fouad Makki reason to favorably view the opening of the Eritrean public sphere during the early days of independence, and Ruth Iyob to be cautiously optimistic about the country's political dynamics around the same time.[41] Despite these

---

40 See relevant Eritrea sections of my book, among many others, *Third World Colonialism and Strategies of Liberation: Eritrea and East Timor Compared* (New York: Cambridge University Press, 2013).

41 See Fouad Makki, "Nationalism, State Formation and the Public Sphere: Eritrea 1991-96," *Review of African Political Economy* Vol. 23, No. 70 (Dec., 1996), 475-497; and Ruth Iyob, "The Eritrean Experiment: A Cautious Pragmatism?" *The Journal of Modern African Studies*, Vol. 35 (4) (December 1997): 647-673.

hopes, the intellectuals and highly skilled professionals (within and without the government) did not build on their proven record of transformative interventions. The jury may still be out on their discovery of a mission as model citizens in the new independent dispensation, and whether they betrayed or fulfilled that mission.[42] The available record indicates their abysmal failure in empowering the people, informing and shepherding policy, and helping usher in civic Eritrea through a healthy but inevitable haggling with political Eritrea, i.e. the state. To the contrary, the majority of them apparently bestowed their powers as citizens – and their responsibility as intellectuals – on the state and placed themselves at the full disposal of the fledgling government.[43]

The educated elite became instant orphans of the newly independent country at the full mercy of the easily aggravated, impatient government of the victors. Armed with effective intelligence, security, media and propaganda apparatuses, the nascent state ultimately sidelined them by piecemeal measures. They were openly scorned by ideologically charged cadres, and shunned by the euphoric public, which cast aspersions on them. With very few exceptions, they lacked access, resources, and the confidence to speak truth to power. Those who braved to do so – Ghirmai Negash's fourth chapter in this volume features only a few of them – and sought to fulfill their responsibilities as citizens and intellectuals were adroitly shown the system's scorn.[44] Whatever the consequences, they faced

---

42 Fanon wrote "Each generation must discover its mission, fulfill it or betray it, in relative opacity." *The Wretched of the Earth*, 145.

43 In Chapter Six of his book, *Eritrea at a Crossroads*, 155ff., Ambassador Andebrhan Welde Giorgis offers a useful exposition of the three core documents that formed the basis of the structures, mandates and goals of the various institutions of the state as they took shape shortly after independence. While those formative documents themselves could not have been produced without the active leadership of the intellectuals and highly skilled professionals, the role of experts in the implementation of those frameworks remained limited. This, perhaps, might have been the principal factor in the structural deformity of the state and floundering of the government in practice.

44 Over several conversations between 2012 and 2017 (in Nairobi), Elias Habte Selassie told me that not all of the educated elite were silent followers, but that the current government had long perfected its craft of silencing critics since the struggle years. He recalls his own questioning of what he found to be unacceptable practices and views until he was sidelined and physically threatened. He relates how on one occasion in

their fate alone. The luckier ones took the caring advice of their well-wishers within the system to err on the side of caution.

A consistent rarity among such individual lone voices in the public sphere has been Wolde-Yesus Ammar, a veteran of the ELF – the rival of the EPLF during the liberation struggle – and an intellectual of remarkable foresight. As early as 1992, he poignantly foretold the risks independent Eritrea faced from the actions and inactions of the victorious independence movement, though many ascribed his stated concerns to the bitterness of someone belonging to an organization that lost in the internecine conflict.[45] Similarly in 1992, my co-author, Ghirmai Negash, gave a powerful lecture to a theater full of mid-level and senior government officials and the public about the need for deliberate nurturing of freedom of expression, and cautioned against complacency, excuses, and scapegoating.[46] Although Ammar was not in the country to face any direct consequences for what he had written, Negash became an object of ridicule and the target of offhand remarks and treatment. He was dismissed as an Amsterdam street smart (because he had at that time come from the Netherlands) by the many who did not know that he too was a veteran of the independence movement and a senior figure at that.

The 1998-2000 conflict with Ethiopia nudged the generation of learned and older Eritreans within the system (and its supporters) to question the prevailing wisdom and point out the perils of not changing course. Whereas Tekie Fessehatzion called for the "Listening to Other Voices" in summer 2000, Saleh AA Younis a year later pointed out the failings of the ruling People's Front for Democracy and Justice (PFDJ) by its own standards, and openly called on it to dissolve itself.[47] Perhaps most historically, in October 2000, thirteen

---

the late 1970s the then EPLF representative in Europe, Andemichael Kahsai, warned him: "a revolutionary sword would be unsheathed on you had you been in the field."

45 Wolde-Yesus Ammar, *Eritrea: Root Causes and War and Refugees* (1992).

46 ግርማይ ነጋሽ፥ "ናይ ደረስቲ ናጽነት፣" ብዕለት 27 ሕዳር 1992 ኣብ ኣስመራ ዝተገብረ ኣስተምህሮ። Ghirmai Negash, "The Freedom of the Writer," a public lecture delivered in Asmara on 27 November 1992. The lecture was originally published as a booklet. It has been translated into English, and published in http://www.warscapes.com/retrospectives/eritrea/freedom-writer.

47 Tekie Fessehatzion, "Is the Cease-fire Holding? Barely, But That's Not bad Considering," July 25, 2000: http://www.dehai.org/conflict/articles/tekie_Cease-fire_Holding_Barely.html; Tekie Fessehatzion,

prominent Eritrean academics and professionals (hence G-13) penned an important document to President Isaias Afwerki, mentioned in the first chapter. Not only did they critically analyze the genesis of the concentration of power but they also blamed it on the leaders' collective failure to resist its early signs.[48] Could all of this have been too little, too late?

Conclusion

Meanwhile, the government enacted decidedly pro-poor and pro-rural top-down socioeconomic and developmental policies in near complete disregard of the urban populations. Without political mechanisms of inclusion that ensured that their voices would be heard and their interests addressed, and without sufficient organizing to push their interests up the policy agenda, the urban population – some in collusion with corrupt officials, others by taking advantage of the rapidly receding state – resorted to a myriad of survivalist practices to thwart the government's heavy hand. The moneyed sectors of the society, for example, drew sustenance from the parallel markets that burgeoned at the same rate that the state-directed economy withered. The depressed government rate of foreign exchange vis-à-vis the black market starved the national economy of foreign hard currency and eroded its vitality. Whatever the official government policy, senior government, ruling party, and military officials are widely believed to have taken active part in what under normal circumstances would be illegal transactions, contraband trade, and tax evasion.

The cost of those policies – or lack of them – continues to be felt across wide swathes of the urban as well as rural populations in Eritrea, especially the young and the educated. Government over-reaction to the slightest citizen actions unsanctioned by the withering state only worsened the situation. As the length of national service started to take

---

"Listening to Other Voices," *Eritrea Profile* (5 August 2000); Saleh AA Younis, "ShaEbia ktHaqiq alewa. PFDJ Should Dissolve Itself," July 2001: http://fp.asmarino.com/Comments/July2001/Saleh_Younis_07-03.asp

48 Variously referred to as "Berlin Manifesto" or "the G-13 letter," the document is now available in the public domain. Also reproduced as "Letter to H.E. Isaias Afwerki," Berlin, October 3, 2000, in Bereket Habte Selassie's *Wounded Nation: How a Once Promising Eritrea was Betrayed an its Future Compromised* (Trenton, NJ and Asmara: The Red Sea Press, 2011), Appendix I, 289-296.

a toll on the youth and their families, sizeable numbers of national-service-age men and women in urban centers either refused to report for mandatory national service or went AWOL from their military units. The government responded with random, forcible pickups of draft dodgers from city streets, and with violent raids of their homes or suspected hiding places. The government often would send them to "rehabilitation" programs for extended duration in subhuman conditions. As rural communities started to feel the pressure as well, their youth in national service also went AWOL to assist their elderly, disabled, or single parents during farming and harvesting seasons. The government's response was no different in the case of rural youth going AWOL; it either found and apprehended them, arrested their parents until their children reported back to duty, or fined the parents with the hefty sum of Nakfa 50,000 (the equivalent of US $3,333 according to government exchange rate at the time). Such draconian state countermeasures – not to mention the inhumane treatment commanding officers meted out to the servicemen and servicewomen without accountability – worsened the situation in Eritrea.

Many of the young and the educated – and, in recent years, the elderly and unaccompanied minors too – voted with their feet, risking humiliation, extreme emotional and physical hardship, and slow torturous death while seeking to flee. Disengaged from their community and society's affairs, many of Eritrea's young created a vicious cycle of looking outward for solutions by fleeing their problems at home. As a result, the government has seen its capacity to deliver on policy pronouncements steadily weaken. This has contributed to rural youth joining the exodus, weakening the country in the present and endangering its future.

The government dismisses the scale of the flight of its nationals as miniscule. Even when acknowledging this as a phenomenon worthy of discussion, the government blames it on foreign detractors. A crucial point is lost in these hardheaded denials: innovation, development, progress, and prosperity usually cannot occur without the free, creative, youthful, rebellious energy of young members of a society. When deprived of the freedom, space, and incentives to succeed and advance sustainably, the most energetic and capable change agents in that society go where they feel they will not be smothered by the state. Refusing to constructively address the flight of Eritrean youth, the government disowned those who fled the country and left them to face their fate. Failing the most basic of responsibilities of an administering authority for even those who fall in line with its diktats, the state leadership now finds itself in one humdrum – even depressing – corner with a growing number of the population congregating in many scattered and cacophonous corners only united by their varying degrees of opposition to the government.

Chapter Four

'WHO, THEN, DO WE DESIRE TO BE?': OPENING CONVERSATIONS ON ERITREA'S POSSIBLE FUTURES

Ghirmai Negash

> Everything, then, starts with an act of identification: 'I am Black.' The act of identification is based on a question that we ask of ourselves: 'Who, then, am I?' … To be black is to be stuck at the foot of a wall with no doors, thinking nonetheless that everything will open up in the end.
> —Achille Mbembe, *Critique of Black Reason*, 151-152.

This essay attempts to deal with the broad question of Eritrea's identity, and what role the nation wants to play as a legitimate member of the African community of nations and the global community at large. But it is chiefly concerned with – and written with the purpose of opening conversations on – the issues that have impacted the construction of the country's sad image most profoundly and persistently, and how their negative consequences might impact its future. As described in the preceding sections of this volume, and by various other critical works, Eritrea's image today is essentially that of an angry, isolated, and alienated African country that is neither at peace with itself nor with the world. And it is also precisely for this reason that the most senior experts on Eritrea such as Bereket Habte Selassie and Kjetil Tronvoll were able to write books with titles containing phrases such as "wounded nation," and "the African garrison state".[1] More worrisome is that, despite this alienation and antagonism, its current rulers continue to perpetuate a self-serving master narrative of Eritrean "exceptionalism". They use it to glorify their own role and achievements of the past as liberators, but also to warp public thinking about the gravity of the current dire situation. During the independence war when the idea of exceptionalism evolved as a slogan, the narrative held that the Eritrean people, despite being deprived of wide recognition and support from the international community, were defiant and capable enough to fight for their right of self-determination, despite and against all odds.[2] In fact, the idea of exceptionalism was never conceived to endorse isolation, but rather referred to the people's determination in the face of seclusion.

Eritrea's experience is extraordinary in many ways, and especially so considering that this small African country of about five million people achieved independence from Ethiopia by defeating massive Ethiopian military campaigns that were alternatingly armed and supported by the United States and the former Soviet Union during the Cold War era. This epic story of resistance, sacrifice, and valor of the Eritrean people in their struggle for self-determination is well documented by some of the ablest historians and journalists, including Eritrean historian Alemseged Tesfai, British-born Basil Davidson, Michela Wrong, and the American writer Dan Connell, who wrote during and after the end of Eritrea's independence struggle of thirty violent years. Yet, the problem with this perpetual hankering for a narrative of uniqueness is that current President Isaias Afwerki exploits it to prolong his own one-party tyranny. The narrative serves the regime in at least three interrelated ways. It is used as a default explanation to legitimize the former liberators turned absolute rulers' self-appointed sense of responsibility to continue ruling the country

---

1   See further Bereket Habte Selassie, *Wounded Nation: How a Once Promising Eritrea was Betrayed and its Future Compromised* (Trenton, NJ: Red Sea Press, 2010); and Kjetil Tronvoll and Daniel R. Mekonnen *The African Garrison State: Human Rights and Political Development in Eritrea* (Rochester, NY: James Currey, 2014).

2   For an examination of an aspect of this, see Awet T. Weldemichael, "African Diplomacy of Liberation: the Case of Eritrea's Search for an 'African India'," *Cahiers d'Études africaines*, Vol. 4, No. 212 (2013/4), 867-894.

indeterminately;[3] to create fear among the citizenry through opening old wounds that make them worry about once again falling victim to Ethiopian re-colonization and U.S. and U.N.-backed international conspiracy; and, finally, to discourage critical conversations about the possibilities of Eritrea's transition to democratic rule. The idea of Eritrean exceptionalism blocks or preempts all other dissenting or competing narratives and voices, including those constructively critical narratives that would have been possible even during the violent years of the armed struggle.

Voices of reason and dissent have been present in both Eritrea's distant and recent history. Ibrahim Sultan and Woldeab Woldemariam, two Founding Fathers of Eritrean nationalism, took heed of the dividing historical circumstances between Eritrean Muslims and Christians in the era (1940s-1950s) in which they lived. Concerned that the birth of Eritrean nationalism would collapse under religious divisions, they arranged a symbolic event by which to convey to the constituencies the importance of unity. In a historical gesture with profound resonances, they came together to share communal Muslim-Christian meals and swore on the two holy books. Woldeab Woldemariam later remembered in a powerful eulogy to his friend and life-long comrade, Ibrahim Sultan,

> Do you remember in 1944, when we met at the residence of Saleh Kekia and symbolically shared a chicken slaughtered by a Muslim, swore upon the Holy Quran, and then proceeded to share a chicken slaughtered by a Christian, and swore upon the Bible to carry out our Eritrea for Eritreans struggle without any religious, regional, ethnic divisions?[4]

In 2001, a group of concerned former ministers and leaders in the Eritrean government known as G-15 expressed their grievances about the monopoly and abuse of power by the current Eritrean president. And so did the four bishops of the Eritrean Catholic Church as extensively discussed in this book.

---

3   The demagogy about endless emergencies and difficulties that the government has to face – and how the leaders were always up to the challenge – is a clear evidence of this. But Eritrea's President has also explicitly expressed his plans to rule the country indefinitely on several occasions.

4   Quoted in Dawit Mesfin, *Woldeab Woldemariam: A Visionary Eritrean Patriot, A Biography* (Trenton, NJ: The Red Sea Press, 2017), 285.

Yet, as someone interested in cultural productions, I also recognize that even during the armed struggle days, signs of concern about the challenges of nation-building were showing up in both the conventional political rhetoric, narratives, and expressions inscribed in cultural artifacts, and the critical and creative literary essays and poems. Of course, always mindful of the constraints imposed by the war and the EPLF's organizational limitations, the writers and artists understandably could not provide direct criticism but rather wrote in anticipation, and always with a sense of ambiguity and indirectness. One might be tempted to wonder what such cultural or literary texts might add to our existing knowledge of the Eritrean revolution. Not very much, if we read them as simple reflections of the reality of the ongoing struggle at the time. But if we read and study them carefully, the hidden voices and subtexts in those artifacts can help one understand the deeper dilemmas and hopes of the Eritrean struggle for freedom and post-war identity of the nation.

The future of Eritrea and its people is ultimately bound with the varied experiences and potential futures of the African peoples at large. No national or ethnic group can build a sustainable future built on isolationism and/or a single theoretical explanation of its own experience, such as in Eritrea's case, a notional interpretation of its own exceptionalism. This being the case, I draw further inspiration from a certain thread of Pan-Africanism so as to contextualize the question of Eritrea's unique history of suffering and struggles. To forge viable national and Pan-African identities for Eritrea, it is necessary that Eritrea's present and future identities are theorized through a Pan-Africanist critique that emerges from a broader understanding of the continent's experience of decolonization. Joining in such productive Pan-Africanist critique can help bring about new ways of thinking that can contribute toward helping the country come in from the cold, where it finds itself momentarily. Despite the unavoidable obsession with our own suffering and struggle for survival and freedom as a people, we should be able to look beyond ourselves; to understand the suffering and struggle of other African brothers and sisters on the continent and across the globe; and to learn from the perspectives developed from those experiences. The vital lessons learned from the discussion can then be transposed to the Eritrean context to ask the most pertinent set of questions that I raise as central to this essay: 'Who Are We as Eritreans in This Contemporary World?'; 'Who, Then, Do We Desire to Be?'. And how do we define our identity in relation to our history, to Africa, to the new and old black diaspora, and eventually the world at large?

Wounded Selfhood in the Clinic of Pan-Africanism

In *Critique of Black Reason* (2017), the Cameroonian historian and philosopher Achille Mbembe opens his sixth chapter, titled "The Clinic of the Subject", by noting the paradoxes of being and becoming in the contemporary world, as an African individual, and as Africans in the collective. As in the rest of the book, the fundamental premise of this chapter is the idea that African identity of difference cannot be ground down to reductionist simplicities, but also that the future of Africa and its peoples must be sought not in separation but rather within a principled commitment to "a larger project – the project of a world that is [be]coming" and "whose destination is universal", even though there is no simple or single path to achieving it.[5] Mbembe's dialogical critique of African history, its ever-evolving identity, and its potential future(s) juxtapose different perspectives to explain the complexities of the African predicament, which he so minutely and powerfully evokes. His text persistently and unapologetically recaps the apocalyptic violence of slavery and (neo)colonialism that, for over four hundred years, conditioned and continues to have great impact on the existential experience of the African peoples.[6] It provides, on the other hand, a sympathetic and thoughtful consideration of the anti-slavery and anti-colonial practical and ideological struggles of the African peoples to recover and reclaim their identity, despite the odds

---

5   Achille Mbembe, *Critique of Black Reason*, trans. Laurent Dubois (Durham and London: Duke University Press, 2017), 183.

6   Important works on the atrocities and impacts of slavery and colonialism in Africa include Joseph Conrad's *Heart of Darkness* (1899); Aimé Césaire, *Discourse on Colonialism* (Monthly Review Press, 2000); and Frantz Fanon's *The Wretched of the Earth* (Grove Press, 1963). For writings by contemporary authors on the same topic see the seminal works by Mahmood Mamdani, *When Victims Become Killers: Colonialism, Nativism, and the Genocide in Rwanda* (Princeton, NJ: Princeton University Press, 2001); Adam Hochschild, *King Leopold's Ghost* (New York, NY: Houghton Mifflin Harcourt, 1999); and Michela Wrong, *In the Footsteps of Mr. Kurtz: Living on the Brink of Disaster in Mobutu's Congo* (New York, NY: New York, NY: HarperCollins Publishers, 2001), and *I Didn't Do It For You: How the World Betrayed a Small African Nation* (HarperCollins Publishers, 2005). Wrong's *I Didn't Do It For You* describes the terrible deeds and long-term impact of British and American Imperialisms specifically in Eritrea.

pitted against them. On the question of identity in the context of the colonial and postcolonial era, he writes that the unmistakable African resolve for the quest and affirmation of identity is a desire for autonomous self-expression. It is also a need born out of necessity to react, to clarify questions around one's postcolonial condition and the imperative to broker a way of coming to terms with the language and ideology of the erstwhile colonizing European Other. For Mbembe, identity is thus inherently formed in the process of exchanging linguistic meanings, through forms of questioning and answering, about lived experiences in a highly charged and contested terrain. The referenced opening lines to Mbembe's chapter read thus:

> Everything, then, starts with an act of identification: 'I am Black.' The act of identification is based on a question that we ask of ourselves: 'Who, then, am I?' Or else it is a response to a question asked of us, a summons: 'Who are you?' In both cases identity is unveiled and made public. But to unveil one's identity is also to recognize oneself. It is a form of self-recognition. It is to know who you are and to speak it or, better, to proclaim it – to say it to oneself. The act of identification is also an affirmation of existence. 'I am' signifies, from that moment forward, 'I exist.'[7]

Mbembe is well known for his stylized élan and his use of metaphysical language as a shorthand. In the quoted passage, the condensed lines alluding to the Cartesian wisdom of doubting and self-doubting ("I think; therefore I am") also pave the ground for connecting the analysis with the haunting questions by Senghor and Césaire that appear later in the chapter when they are quoted by him asking themselves and the world: "Who are we in this white world?"[8] Mbembe, like his predecessors, writes in a genealogy of "a long line of Black intellectual criticism that can be found among African-American as well as Anglophone Caribbean and African thinkers",[9] including Marcus Garvey, Aimé Césaire, Frantz Fanon, Léopold Sédar Senghor, and Langston Hughes, all of whom the Cameroonian author resuscitates and reinterprets, making their work pertinent to contemporary scholarship and readers. Despite the theoretical project of the book and the sophisticated intertextualities of various European, African, and black strands of thought that are identified and

---

7   Mbembe, *Critique of Black Reason*, 151.
8   Ibid., 159.
9   Ibid., 157.

woven together to make his arguments, Mbembe also knows we live in a real and hostile world today. The unfolding events in the United States, where black lives do not seem to matter, and the sub-humanization of African refugees (many of them from Eritrea but also from other African countries) in Mediterranean and European countries are – though not directly mentioned – in his purview. It is significant, too, that the actual terms used by the preceding intellectuals and writers, particularly by Senghor and Césaire, to formulate the African search for identity reverberate and find new meaning and urgency in Mbembe's text. Mbembe clearly has no wish in his book to remain silent or "shy away" from the difficult questions of colonialism, racism, and stigmatism about which, following Césaire, he affirms that these "remain today for the most part unanswered".[10] It appears in fact that while creating a deep critical knowledge, providing conceptual tools, and charting the trajectories of Pan-Africanist thinking in coping with the legacies of colonialism, he also sees himself as part of that inquiry. His wounded postcolonial being is an object of inspection under the telescopic gaze of Pan-Africanist theories that he essentially uses to function as the "Clinical" underpinning for examining the lives and struggles of the African "Subject". This underlying impulse is manifested in the various ways he interlaces the personal, the communal, and the universal in his narrative. But it is more plainly expressed when he writes at one point in "The Clinic of the Subject": "'Black' is the name that was given to me by someone else. I did not choose it… 'Black' is the person who cannot look the Other straight in the Eye. To be black is to be stuck at the foot of a wall with no doors, thinking nonetheless that everything will open up in the end".[11]

In this essay, I want to embrace Mbembe's stance and reflections on African and black identity as mine. From the perspective of Eritrean selfhood, which is fractured, wounded, directionless, and sliding down the misguided path of isolationism, the above picture provides a critical space from which we can explore new directions informed by it, while simultaneously drawing cultural elements from our own experience as a portal to inform the future. More importantly, I want to appropriate his ("Who, then, am I?") and Césaire's ("Who are we in this white world?"), and raise these questions with reference to Eritrea. With a slight grammatical twist and contextual re-framing, the duo's pertinent question – and its deeper underlying concerns –

---

10   Ibid.
11   Ibid., 151-152.

can be transposed to and asked in the Eritrean context. Thus: "Who, then, are we Eritreans as citizens and subjects of a 'wounded' nation in this contemporary world?" And "Who, then, do we desire to be?" To say it in a more direct way: How do we define our identity in relation to our history, in relation to Africa, and by extension to the new and old black diaspora – and the world at large? Can we, for example, unequivocally embrace our African-ness without being consumed by a sense of alienation suffered in the name of exceptionalism? It neither makes up for the loss of identity nor provides real substance for building mature alternatives for self-identification. Alternatively, can we develop different images about ourselves and the country by, for example, tapping into our useful and usable past constructively?

Behind Exceptionalism: The Wound and the Cure

Bernard M. Magubane, in his critically acclaimed book, *The Ties That Bind: African-American Consciousness of Africa* (1987, 1994), quotes Max Weber's theory of the formation of group identity and the sense of pride centering on the differences between privileged and disadvantaged communities. Weber describes the difficulty of disadvantaged groups, which he calls the "negatively privileged", as a condition of trauma and damage engendered by their deprived socio-economic and political status. Weber also presents a hypothesis about the possible strategy that is available for these groups to develop, something they must have for their survival and, perhaps, triumph. According to Weber:

> The sense of dignity that characterizes positively privileged status groups is naturally related to their 'being' which does not transcend itself; that is, it is to their 'beauty' and excellence. Their kingdom is 'of this world.' They live for the present and by exploiting the great past. The sense of dignity of the negatively privileged strata naturally refers to a future lying beyond the present whether it is of this life or of another. In other words, it must be nurtured by a belief in a providential 'mission' and by a belief in a specific honor before God.[12]

Eritrean nationalism and sense of exceptionalism is not built on religious foundations. While Christianity and Islam, the two main

---

12 Quoted in Bernard M. Magubane, *The Ties That Bind: Afro-American Consciousness of Africa* (Trenton, NJ: Africa World Press, 1994), 7.

religions of the country, have exerted strong influences on the formation of Eritrean embryonic nationalism,[13] the sense of national exceptionalism that has evolved over the years is a form of secularized exceptionalism, neither driven by a belief in any specific religious conviction nor deity, in a strictly Weberian sense. Nonetheless, Weber's citing a preordained, fated "mission", of living and working toward achieving or serving a higher purpose than a community's actual situation would permit, is also somewhat applicable to what can be properly identified as Eritrean secularized exceptionalism. This is by virtue of its disconnect from lived reality and its mystified associations with some kind of extraordinary nature and destiny, none of which has ever been explained by anyone in logical terms and ways comprehensible to the public. But how did the Eritrean sense of exceptionalism manifest itself? What were its origins, and what is behind it today? In other words, what purpose did it serve historically, and what is its motivation and function at present?

The notion of exceptionalism has meant different things and served different purposes in Eritrean history. During the war of independence, the main propaganda conceived and disseminated by the nationalist movements and leaders centered on the country's unique history and status of being an "exceptional colony". In some ways, it shared a similar European colonial history with other colonized African countries but also distinguished itself by being an African brand of Ethiopian colonization. Official media outlets and seminars also widely speculated that Eritrea's anomalous status was in fact its source of strength. Keen on blaming others and always self-justifying for policy errors, the EPLF elite leaders in particular skillfully explained to their combatants and civilian supporters that international rejection indeed vindicated their determination to go it alone, despite and against all odds. Not only that. Although the Eritrean revolution was neither the first nor the only independence movement of its kind in Africa, there was a concerted effort to claim that the struggle was incomparable to any other in its motives and methods and that the Eritrean people fought colonialism differently – and more efficiently – than all other armed struggles on the African continent. Such myth of unparalleled Eritrean heroism and strategic vision, as told and repeated by its leaders to help win the independence war, continued after the

---

13 See, for example, Joseph L. Venosa, *Paths Toward the Nation: Islam, Community, and Early Nationalist Mobilization in Eritrea, 1941-61* (Athens: Ohio University Press, 2014).

country's independence. Most civilians – indoctrinated by the former freedom fighters turned government leaders – uncritically, and even assertively, subscribed to the consummate myth of the revolution. The mystification sometimes took the form of maintaining that the experience of the Eritrean struggle was too complex and unique to be told by individual historians and other writers, but rather could only be narrated by the state-operated newspaper and the national television (Eri-TV) that, in a fit of supreme irony, called itself the "Source of Truth".

One consequence was discouraging individual narratives about the fight for independence. As the myth about the armed struggle crystallized into shape, many former combatants could not write their stories independently. They feared that any attempt to write history would not dovetail with the official myth that had nurtured them but about which they now felt intimidated and deceived. However, a few who did attempt to write their memoirs drew severe criticism from the state media, which accused them variably of individualism, polemics, and sacrilege.[14] At other times, the government angrily denounced those journalists and writers who had the temerity to not repeat or maintain the myth. In 2001, a clear example of this conflict between contending "truths" ended in terminal confrontation when the government shut down the seven private newspapers and arrested a dozen journalists working for them. The state leveled baseless charges of anti-patriotism and dissemination of false information about internal political opposition and the country.

During the independence struggle and several years in the post-independence era, the myth of exceptionalism had served Eritrea in both positive and negative terms. It helped mobilize the masses, instigating empowerment during the darkest hours of their struggle for self-determination. Yet, it also gave the political leadership the opportunity to consolidate its narrow ideology and cultivate undemocratic culture and power structures. This ultimately led to repression and the post-independence betrayal of the national-democratic revolution for which thousands gave their time and energy, and in many cases their lives. The leadership's control over and manipulation of its members and supporters came about partly by virtue of the fact that, during the armed struggle, most of its participants did not have access to the outside world. Even today most

---

14   Abraham T. Zere, review of *Kab Rix' Ḥafnti*, by Tekie Beyene, *Journal of Eritrean Studies* VI, no. 1 (2012): 149-156.

Eritreans remain victims of state-driven propaganda until when and if they succeed in leaving their confined Eritrean spaces. Average Eritreans still think their country is much more civilized, modernized, and in many ways superior to most other African countries. Some members of the ruling elite and self-appointed guardians in the Eritrean diaspora have come to think that "their" government and the Eritrean people can do anything, including create a new world (dis)order, if they want. Others take it to a still higher level and can be heard boasting of their unique identity as if they were superior to other African ethnicities and races. As has been reported by various commentators, the Eritrean capital, Asmara, which is renowned for its colonial architectural beauty, has played and continues to play a significant role in the myth-creation of exceptionalism.

Sociologist Tekle Woldemikael, an Eritrean professor at Chapman University in Southern California, has attempted to trace the genealogy of Eritrean ethno-racialism by describing how the intersecting effects of primeval sentiments, social hierarchy, and history led to its rise. He writes,

> Although Eritreans cannot and do not see themselves in terms of clearly defined races as in the West or the United States, the social relations between one another are based on exclusion and mythology of a purity based on family genealogy lineages where such genealogy and lineages are said to be free from assumed 'slave' lineages or membership in a caste group in society. Religion, regional belonging, and an oral history of origins determine the boundaries as well as the intermixing of the groups that evolved over a long period of time to form what we now consider ethno-racial groups. This cultural ideology of inclusion and exclusion, belonging and not belonging also becomes the organizing principle of social relations among Eritreans and Ethiopians, Eritreans and other Africans, and others. The Eritrean identity is constructed from principles of social relations that intersect and merge with the supposed uniqueness of Eritrean history as a crossroads of the Middle East, Africa, and the antiquity of the region, as well as the recent history of Italian colonialism (1890-1941), British occupation (1941-1952), and Ethiopian federation and annexation (1952-1991).[15]

---

15 Tekle M. Woldemikael, "Eritrea's Identity as a Cultural Crossroads," in *Race and Nation: Ethnic Systems in the Modern World*, ed. Paul R. Spickard (New York and London: Routledge, 2005), 350.

According to Woldemikael, however, this worldview also has been consciously cultivated by the Eritrean intellectual elite and the country's political leadership during the independence struggle and in the post-independence era. He writes that, at a fundamental level, most Eritrean elites and government officials shared in their conception of uniqueness. For example, they overtly touted the idea by advertising the exquisiteness of physical spaces to make their point.

> [T]he differences that often impressed journalists [visiting the country] was what they saw as a more advanced lifestyle when they visited the peaceful, clean, and modern style streets of Asmara, a city built by Italians when they had Eritrea under their control for sixty years. Eritrean elites and government officials also played an active role in nurturing the praises and opinions aired in the mass media about their being more advanced or better than other Africans. To illustrate this, they stressed the cleanliness of Asmara, as well as the fact that it was well-ordered and crimeless, and the ideology of self-reliance of the Eritrean government. They publicly emphasized the perceived difference of their country from other African countries, and thus its uniqueness in Africa.[16]

In the same article, Woldemikael also reveals something that is fundamentally hidden behind the adulatory visitor's optic that the Eritrean authorities like to see magnified. He offers the following astute observations explaining how the image is exploited and why:

> This sense of uniqueness has continued in the self-presentation of the current Eritrean state and its political leadership. However, the Eritrean cultural ideology of uniqueness hides the unresolved and unarticulated conflict of power, and the violent history of the various ethno-racial and religious groups in Eritrea. The lack of an institutionalized resolution of power conflicts and a history of violence lead to continued outbursts of violent confrontation and expression based on the mythology of uniqueness. This may be detrimental to Eritrea and Eritreans who need to live and benefit from a life in a pluralistic and interdependent region. Their neighbors are also embedded in their own local mythologies, which are similar but not identical to those of the Eritreans. (...) Eritrean nationalists' benign search for an identity, which they could call as their own, has led them to desire an identity based on national

---

16   Ibid.

uniqueness [and this] signifies Eritreans' sparse and weak grasp of their history.[17]

Speaking of Eritrean nationalism and exceptionalism is a delicate matter. However, it is more meaningful to approach Eritrean nationalism by critically diagnosing both its empowering and limiting pitfalls so that its dangers are laid bare for examination. A particular African philosophical notion is deeply etched in the Tigrinya saying, "those who hide their wound, hide their cure" (*QusLom Zihab'uu: FewSom Yehab'uu*). This important indigenous notion suggests that not only should the sufferers take responsibility for their suffering, identify it, diagnose it, and find ways of healing, but also recognizes that, if the sufferers fail to do so, they would succumb to it. Eritreans have a reputation for being strong sufferers by virtue of successive colonial and domestic oppressions. But they also will need to develop realistic conceptions of themselves in order to heal from their wounds and recover from the calamitous conditions of oppression under which they continue to live as traumatized people.

If the global image of Eritrea as an angry and isolated nation ruled by totalitarianism is to end, Eritreans must understand that this picture cannot be altered without a vigorous, critical engagement to demystify the distorted image they have of themselves as a separate and exclusive people. Conceived and perpetuated by the founders of the current Eritrean regime to serve their narrow self-interest of retaining power, the duplication of uniqueness and exceptionalism only breeds delusion of grandeur, and an unending cycle of paranoia, self-pity, fear, and mistrust – a deadly cocktail that erodes any healthy sense of belonging both at the national and international levels. The ruling elite's manipulative history and continued tactics to promote exceptionalism have done an exceptional job of legitimizing the terrible deeds of the existing tyranny. If not corrected, the continuation of this egregious historical conditioning will perpetuate the status quo.

Between and Beyond the Borderlines of Exceptionalism: Alternative Voices

Although the above-sketched master narrative of "exceptionalism" has dominated (and continues to dominate) the Eritrean political and cultural landscape, it is important to recognize and acknowledge those Eritreans whose ideas and vision for future Eritrean identity were not

---

17 Ibid., 350-351.

(or are not) entirely constrained/controlled by the political leadership's narrow nationalism and, in fact, have gone beyond its confines to provide alternative voices.

In the 1980s, for example, a new breed of writers and artists born out of the struggle were producing a new kind of literature, music, and critical and creative essays. They primarily wrote for the nationalist cause of the Eritrean struggle, and the source and inspiration of their work was the revolution itself. Working in a war zone, the group operated under the tight discipline and direction of their commanders, and perhaps were not entirely aware of the many subtle yet important ways their work deviated from the main propaganda narrative. Nonetheless, even in this vulnerable and tenuous situation, they as individuals clearly were driven by their desire and ability to create culture and art. They also were accomplished enough to work past the borderlines of the official rhetoric of the revolution to produce a complex blend of patriotic, internationalist, and humane cultural ideology.

Some members of the group were Western-educated intellectuals, writers, and performers who had knowledge of European languages and cultures. One highly visible icon among those figures was University of Wisconsin-educated Alemseged Tesfai. Having survived harsh internal denunciation and alienation within the EPLF organization, he rose to become the organization's literary and cultural architect. He wrote plays, fiction, essays, and in 1988 a seminal critical work entitled *Literature, Its Development, and Its Role in Revolution*. A manifesto that hugely influenced the formative stages of the Eritrean resistance literature during the years of struggle for independence, *Literature, Its Development, and Its Role in Revolution* discusses Eritrean literature by contextualizing, linking, and critiquing it within the scope of European, Russian, African, and African-American literatures. While the rise and fall of classical Greek and Roman literatures are deliberated, it also engages in a useful discussion of anti-colonial, anti-slavery, and other progressive texts by African and African-American writers (including Ghana's Kwame Nkrumah, Kenya's Jomo Kenyatta, South Africa's Peter Abrahams, and W.E.B. Dubois). Drawing inspiration from Ezekiel Mphalele's *The African Image*, Alemseged Tesfai advises his compatriot writers that much wisdom can be learned from "African-bred cultural and ideological concepts such as

Nkrumah's 'African humanism' and Nyerere's 'African socialism'".[18] Tesfai also speaks to Sédar Senghor's notion of "negritude" movement in his critique, but dismisses him offhand. The lack of enthusiasm for Senghor's thinking apparently was because Tesfai, then writing as a Marxist critic, did not see the intersectionality of nationalism, race, and social class. By contrast, Tesfai is full of admiration for Achebe's *Things Fall Apart*, which he views "as a gateway to modern African literature". He particularly finds Ngugi wa Thiong'o's work as a perfect embodiment of revolutionary literature that is congruent with his own Marxian ideal about what a class-driven and emancipatory literature should look like. Tesfai further, and conclusively, touts Ngugi's work as a model for writing a Marxist-oriented, Eritrean revolutionary literature.

But not all of the advice that Alemseged Tesfai proffered to Eritrean writers during the armed struggle was orthodox Marxist. His brand of Marxist or Socialist Realist literature was rather liberal. He foresaw the inevitable risk of placing too much faith in any fixed ideological construct. As I argued when writing *A History of Tigrinya Literature in Eritrea* (1999), a careful reading of his *Literature, Its Development, and Its Role in Revolution* reveals that, while he was hugely impacted by Marxist ideology, he did not see that conviction as inexorably antithetical to individual freedom and creativity. In the text, this is apparent in the section where he denounces facile perceptions of literature that mistake it for "reportage", and summons his compatriots to see themselves as the painter who seizes deep thought in colors and contours, to represent the essence in all its complexity. The task of the writer, he reasons, is,

> Just like the painter who provides a wonderful artistic work by combining colours, and his developed skills of sketching, painting, brushing, and touching, the writer too can give life to the essence of a particular object or event by the composition of words, grammatical effectiveness, and detailed and deep observations.[19]

In the chaotic world of war, death, and existential uncertainty, it may seem that Alemseged Tesfai's aesthetic pronouncement would have sounded eccentric, erratic, unbelievable, and even impossible to experiment with. How could, for example, a hemorrhaging body and

18   Ghirmai Negash, *A History of Tigrinya Literature in Eritrea* (Leiden: CNWS-University of Leiden, 1999), 182.
19   Ibid.,184.

soul of a writer entrenched in battle dugouts find the muse to paint a full and profound image (that is, as Alemseged Tesfai recommends, "to put down detailed and deep observations") of his surroundings with impartiality, and without concealing or obscuring the terrible truths of his riveting subjectivity? To put the same question somewhat differently, when endorsing both the aesthetic and the political, was not Tesfai raising the bar too high for himself and his group of fighter-writers on the frontline? For any writer, this does not seem an easy task to accomplish. American journalist Dan Connell, referring to Tesfai's work years later, remarked that at the very least, "This is no mean feat for any author, but it is especially unusual for one coming out of a political culture of personal silence, where individuals do not make a practice of revealing what goes on within their movement, their unit, let alone their person".[20]

Connell was commenting on Tesfai's collection of essays written during the armed struggle, and published in translation in the volume *Two Weeks in the Trenches* (2002). These narratives of "pain and humiliation, both personal and political; of abiding strength and indomitable courage, also at once personal and political; of wrenching decisions large and small forced on people by the terrible conditions in which they lived and died", writes Connell, "showcase Alemseged as a writer of diverse talents and insights on many levels … and Alemseged's and Eritrea's long and difficult journey to liberation".[21] Connell adds that "the experience that undergirds them and the vision thus generated remain a beacon for all who love liberty and equality and who cherish the common humanity of those who yet strive for them".[22]

Reading one of the stories, entitled *Heart of Tegadalai* ("The Heart of a Struggler", 1988), Connell empathizes with author Alemseged Tesfai as the latter is tortured by the discovery of a still beating human heart lying on the battleground. A tattered jacket lies a short distance away from the bleeding heart, but no identifiable body that can be related to it. The heart could have been of anyone, of an Eritrean freedom fighter or of an enemy.[23] There was no way to tell "of its

---

20 Alemeged Tesfai, *Two Weeks in the Trenches* (Trenton, NJ: Africa World Press, 2002), vi. The essays in this collection were originally written in the Tigrinya language. *Two Weeks in the Trenches* was translated by the author himself.
21 Ibid., vi.
22 Ibid., xii.
23 Ibid., 132.

origins, sex, religion, age, rank, or whether its owner had been a veteran or a novice".[24] Unable to give it 'flesh or face', the writer gives up "bothering about its exact identity", though thinking it might be "the heart of a patriot, the heart of *tegadalai*".[25] He adds that, whatever the case, "I have neither the words nor the space to tell its story, explain its bravery and relay its message. Had I been a poet or a painter, I would probably have said more".[26]

Despite the self-effacement, the author of *Two Weeks in the Trenches* manages to produce one of the most beautifully complex and humane documents that ever emerged from the independence movement. The terror, sorrow, and acrimony around him are weaved together into a formidable narrative of compassion and human solidarity, through threading metaphors associated with the "fallen heart". In the collection, Tesfai pays tribute to the thousands of young men and women of Eritrea who risked their lives – and sometimes sacrificed them – for the ideals of independence, peace, and normalcy.[27] We must remember that the war with Ethiopia was raging while he was writing. But, in a most remarkable turn, he also humanizes the Ethiopian soldiers in the war, even though they are fighting against his side. The striking juxtaposition of the personal ethos, nationalist motto, and humanist values in the paragraphs of *Two Weeks in the Trenches* amplify both the author's mighty talent as a writer and his commitment to a broadminded approach to art and life. Obviously, for Alemseged Tesfai, war, killing, and defiance formed part of the Eritrean identity necessitated by the struggle, but these things never were (and never should have been allowed) to be the enduring representations of the Eritrean people as, unfortunately, the present ruling elite of the country has indeed made them. For Tesfai, the country's independence was a legitimate cause to die for, but precisely because of that, it was also absolutely necessary to recognize the high price that Eritreans, including himself, had to pay in order to overcome the Ethiopian state and defeat its military so they could live without war and its ugly legacies. He writes:

> So, I felt it would be unfair to be satisfied with a mere report of a battle and all the cruelty and abnormality that characterize it… Our

---

24   Ibid.
25   Ibid.
26   Ibid.
27   See Ibid., 133.

revolutionary culture is still very poor in discussing and describing individuals and individual acts of courage and heroism. Unless we do that, the *tegadalai* will never get his due, and his or her greatness will never be known. We keep using very general and lofty terms to define the collective. One hears about perseverance, tenacity, grit and fortitude as characterizing the spirit of *tegadelti*. I find such words extremely limiting and an obstacle to describing what the life of *tegadelti* constitutes. There is no life in those words, no pain... and pain in all its forms – the process of overcoming or suppressing it – is what makes the *tegadalai*. True, the corpses in front of me were the result of the unflinching courage of my comrades, the courage to jump into the lion's den and tackle him by hand. What about the pain, though? The deaths, the fears denied, the hatred for blood, the compassion even for the enemy?[28]

In another passage, where he foresees the dangers of the leadership betraying the people and their cherished ideals and values developed in the revolution, he states:

It is a big one then, this heart of *tegadalai;* and because adversity, fortitude and the flames of war have fomented it into maturity, it has reached a new height. However, it will need careful handling especially in this, its moments of victory, lest it get intoxicated with glory, forget what it has gone through, swell out of proportion and just blow up. ... [A] heart without a guide may prove fickle and flighty and we will need to cultivate, expand, educate and make it wise. A product of the people, it was nurtured by the people. In return, it has shed tears of blood for them. It has fallen for their sake. It is, therefore, incumbent upon this heart to tune its beat with theirs, to preserve their culture and protect their honor, to understand their problems and seek solutions for them. It has the obligation to approach them, not from an attitude of superiority and disdain but with modesty and humbleness. *Above all, we have the duty to guarantee that it renews its oath and lives up to its responsibility never to assume the role of dispenser of freedom and never to ride over its own people.*[29]

Poets Speaking

If Alemseged Tesfai, as a theorist and fiction writer, was the leading figure who set the standard of a progressive and humanist cultural ideology during the national liberation era, other resistance poets had

---

28   Ibid., 117.
29   Ibid., 134-35. Emphasis added.

similar voices. Writing like Tesfai under the auspices of the EPLF in 1989, the poet Isaias Tsegai has a Tigrinya poem rendered in English as "I Am Also a Person". Tsegai was wounded in the war, and he remained active producing poetry and plays during the war and after the country's independence. During the war years, he worked with other poets and critics in the promotion of Eritrean literature and art and was one of the key members who organized and juried literary contests. He co-authored the *Critical Assessment of the Third Literary Competition* (1988), an important cultural document emerging from the movement's Department of Culture. In the post-independence era, Tsegai assumed several responsibilities as a director of a theatre group, poet, and songwriter, and unlike many of his compatriot poets who chose silence, he continued to play the role of a vocal figure on a range of social and cultural matters, until his untimely death in 2012.

In "I Am Also a Person", he describes the pains of an Eritrean freedom-fighter who, invisible to and short of recognition by an "imagined" outside world, calls for recognition and acknowledgement of his identity. In a seeming reworking of the famous lines of the African-American poet Langston Hughes, "I, Too, Am America"/ "I am the darker brother", he declares that even if the world cared less and he "was stripped of everything … And beaten like a slave/Less than human", he still belonged to humanity, too, as *'a person, as an Eritrean'*.[30] Feelings of abandonment and neglect by the international community (coded with the word "world" in the first line of the poem) toward the Eritreans and the loss of "all sense of peace except in saying *I am also a person. I'm an Eritrean*" refer to a perennial sense of bitterness about being forgotten. Alongside that resentment, however, is also the awareness that rejects a relegation of one's identity to an unproductive sense of self-pity and endless desperation. The resentment, in other words, does not interfere with solidarity and humanity but rather is a

---

30   The first seven lines of the opening stanza read as follows:
When I saw the world didn't care
If I was stripped of everything,
Even my dignity,
And beaten like a slave
Less than human,
I lost all sense of peace except in saying
I am also a person. I'm an Eritrean. (Emphasis in original.)
Quoted in Charles Cantalupo and Ghirmai Negash (trans. and eds.), *Who Needs a Story? Contemporary Eritrean Poetry in Tigrinya, Tigre and Arabic* (Asmara: Hidri Publishers, 2005), 9.

temporary self-consolation and self-affirmation, both necessary to escape death, to continue the journey under circumstances of war and violence. In this respect, it is also remarkable that in the second stanza, the poet focuses not so much on his national identity (Eritrean-ness, which he takes for granted) as on the fragility of his physical body when faced with mortality. He reminds readers that, after all, "With death so close/I wished I was never born/But I still said, *I am also a person*".[31] As we recall from Mbembe's axiom quoted in the beginning of this chapter, "the act of [self-]identification" also entails the "making public" of one's identity. And so while the world's rejection of his identity as defined by specific circumstances has hurt the poet, his belonging to common humanity is affirmed precisely by the act of his declaration as a feeling and reasoning human being. This is despite the extraordinary challenges defining his bare survival. In the poem, we also see that the poet rejects the permanence of hostility; not only is the horror ("Nothing but drought ahead/Or the angel of death/Nothing but one horror/Pouring over another") explained and contextualized but also the unsustainable mayhem and dismay are wished away. The poet's hopeful eyes see the unavoidably huge sacrifices that have been made – death, physical and mental injuries, exposure to extreme heat and cold compounded by hunger (see second stanza) – leading to freedom and liberty in the post-independence era. He writes that he fought for this country because "I loved this country/I wanted it back" (see stanzas seven and eight), and because he believed in the reward, "Peace, progress, and freedom", for all in the freed nation.[32]

"A Candle for the Darkness" (1988),[33] another remarkable poem, by Ghirmai Ghebremeskel, reinforces the view that the fight for Eritrea's freedom was worthwhile because it would culminate in achieving freedom and liberty for its people. A senior veteran of

---

31 "I am Also a Person," lines 12-14.

32 The last stanza reads thus:
I wanted it back
If I endured
I would get my reward.
Peace, progress and freedom
Began with those words.
Clenching my teeth, I had to tell myself.
I am also a person. I'm an Eritrean.

33 *Who Needs a Story? Contemporary Eritrean Poetry in Tigrinya, Tigre and Arabic*, 59-63.

notable talent, Ghebremeskel wrote extensively during the independence struggle, and after independence edited the first anthology of Eritrean poetry, *Mezmur Tegadalai* (1992). In "A Candle for the Darkness", Ghebremeskel, like Tsegai, speaks to his audience from a space of a vicious violence: "When every day / is nothing but death / and more death / hunger and more hunger / war and more war".[34] Drawing on a religious but somehow secularized variety of "sacrifice" that dying for one's nation is not dying but "sacrificing" (fifth stanza), he asks his compatriots to gift their bodies to the nationalist revolution. Using contrastive metaphors of "light and darkness", he describes them as carriers of the burning candle ("Accept this candle and go").[35] The distinctions between torch and torch-carrier nonetheless coalesce when the poet works the internal tensions of the poem to their inevitable conclusion that the militants were actually the physical embodiments of the candle. "Sacrific[e] yourself, like the candle", he writes.[36] What would be the reward for the sacrifice? Why should people be asked to die for a future that they will not see, be part of, simply because they will die?

According to this poet, the benefit of the revolution was rather to future generations. In lines equally lyrical, optimistic, and visionary, he writes that he can see the better times when the people will not be "haunted by devils and death" and when the "birds will sing again".[37] Popular participation, solidarity, and unity were the virtues with which the Eritrean nationalist movement prided itself and which ultimately brought independence. During the war, a variety of forms of cultural entertainment, political, and academic events and celebrations were organized inside the country and in the diasporic communities. While providing the movement with huge sums of money and moral support, these political and cultural activities also raised the movement's profile internally and globally as grassroots supported effort. The poet Ghebremeskel is aware in his piece of the importance of honoring the promises of the revolution as a popular movement.

He knows the mobilization and participation of the masses will be as critical for the postcolonial reconstruction of the country as it had been during the struggle years. He expresses his hope in the poem that, as with the war for independence, the post-independence rebuilding

---

34   Ibid., 59 (stanza 4).
35   Ibid., (stanza 2).
36   Ibid., (stanza 5).
37   Ibid., 61 (stanzas 8 and 9).

of the country will involve the broad participation and dedication of all good-willing citizens, who will be "coming from all directions". The connotation of the words "from all directions" in the poem further suggests that the poet hoped the country would benefit from perspectives emerging from the diverse experiences and leadership know-how of Eritreans in different fields (not just the former combatants!). The poem makes clear, moreover, with phrases such as "joining together in one hall", that he simultaneously hoped that the incumbent ruling elite of the country would welcome participation by varied individuals and political forces. Given the ill-advised ambition of the ruling elite to create a totalitarian state excluding all other forces and voices, Ghebremeskel's optimistic vision sadly remains today as only a reminder of what could have been had the country taken the poet's intended course of governance. The lines in which the poet envisioned Eritrea's pathway to victory in its war of independence, just as in its successful transformation to a post-independence democratic society based on people's participation, read as follows.

> I see these days
> When the horror will end,
> And our future like a candle
> Comes out of the darkness
> And lights up the horizon
> Brimming with people
> Marching into the light—
> Candles and more candles
> Coming from all directions,
> Giving each other their flame
> And joining together in one hall.[38]

Opening Conversations on Eritrea's Possible Futures

Are there realistic and non-violent ways by which the current Eritrean political status quo of totalitarianism and international alienation can be changed and replaced by a people's government that is based on democratic participation of its people, at peace with themselves and the outside world? That is what many Eritreans and external observers have been asking for the past few years. There are ways by which the current reputation of an angry and isolated nation ruled by totalitarianism can be redressed. But it is important first to acknowledge a few things in order to pave the way for analytical clarity.

---

38   Ibid., 61-63.

First: Although the EPLF (later renamed PFDJ) came to power in Eritrea with various unresolved political issues inherited from the time of the armed struggle, it started in the right direction as a government when it took power in the 1990s. Some of the positive measures taken by the ruling party and its government included infrastructural projects targeted at mending and building roads, dam projects, and the reorganization and setting up of clinics and schools especially designed to benefit the rural populations. Ideologically, it also appeared that the government was keen to create an atmosphere of political diversity and inclusivity in limited ways, and even seemed to accept the idea of elections based on a constitution ratified in 1997 by the then existing but later terminated constituent assembly. The attainments of the first six years or so of this stage included plans or projects to rehabilitate the former combatants; facilitate the return of refugees; regularize civilian life; and normalize relations with neighboring countries, including Ethiopia. In the realm of culture and education, the school and university curricula were restored and upgraded to meet global standards; plenty of workshops, symposia, and conferences were organized to boost Eritrean languages, literatures, music, and generally the arts. These achievements and activities were variously reported by ordinary visitors and professional journalists who visited the country in those first seven years or so (1991-1997).

Second: However, it is also important to admit (especially by those who still defend or apologize for the system) that the ruling government's net record has been disgraceful. The first serious sign of problems showing the government's flaws manifested when the Eritrean army, astonishingly, decided to crush a peaceful protest of its own disabled war veterans in 1994, in Mai Habar, maiming and killing a few of them in cold blood. General abuse of human rights and imprisonment and disappearance of the regime's opponents has continued regularly over the years.

The worst of the bloodletting in post-independence Eritrea occurred in 1998-2001 when Eritrea and Ethiopia once again engaged in a tragic and costly war – this time in a border conflict, avoidable if it had been properly handled – causing the loss of many thousands of lives on both sides, including about 20,000 Eritreans, mostly young men and women. In its deadly mixture of epic bloodshed, subsequent economic hardship, war-related trauma, and demoralization of the population, the border conflict engendered further consequences. Discontented top government officials rebelled against the president, accusing him of autocracy and mismanagement of the war, and in 2001 created a faction called G-15. The newspapers existing at the time published widely read articles airing the views of the dissidents and independent writers. This inflamed existing differences within the leadership, with all sides petitioning their grievance through the newspapers. The bitter online and offline campaigns exacerbated the already combustible political landscape. President Isaias Afwerki amassing support from his internal group of loyalists and the army, as he always did when faced with dissent, finally crushed the opposition in September 2001. He arrested the opposition leaders, jailed journalists, and banned private newspapers. This dashed the last hopes of building a society in which alternative voices and some form of liberal politics and public discourse would play a role, quite literally turning the clock back to where Eritrea had started.

When one thinks about Eritrea today, the sad fact is that not only have the achievements of the early years of independence not been sustained, but the future looks bleaker than ever before. The country's economic, political, and moral regression has been identified and reported by plenty of critics and observers. This includes, significantly, the brave Eritrean bishops who, putting their theological faith to the service of liberation, charted the country's economic, political, and moral decline in "Where Is Your Brother?" in 2014, the critical document that inspired the writing of this book.

Three years since publication of "Where Is Your Brother?", the deteriorating situation seems to have worsened. Twenty years after the ratification of the 1997 national constitution, any lingering prospects of its implementation have practically died. Meanwhile, the country's president and his ruling party have declared their desire to substitute the legally endorsed constitution with a bogus constitution of their own. Eritreans continue to flee the country in droves, often taking huge risks reminiscent of the Lampedusa tragedy of 2013 (in which more than 360 Eritreans drowned, under circumstances widely discussed elsewhere, and in this book). Political arrests of individuals and groups continue, while the international media, including the BBC, New Yorker and New York Times, report stories of terrible acts of torture, being buried alive, and suicide in the many prisons and detention centers spread across Eritrea.

Meanwhile, opposition activists and political parties, as well as critically minded supporters of the regime, remain divided between and among themselves on how to come to terms with their country's predicament. Seemingly unable to entertain broader venues and ways of resolving the national problem, most opposition elements and parties appear pathetically satisfied with their own distinctive ethnic, religious, regional, and provincial political identities. These are forces that, instead of divisiveness and infighting, should have mobilized their resources to forge democratic alliances to prevent Eritrea from being destroyed further by the totalitarian elite in power. Similarly, those who support or sympathize with the regime – but yet are concerned about the future of the country – apologetically adhere to the regime's nationalist narrative of Eritrea's unique historical situation, instead of doing anything to prevent the hard-won independence from being further squandered by the vain and reckless leadership of President Isaias Afwerki and his ruling party. The bottom line is that regardless of their real and perceived differences, those Eritreans of good will and democratic principles should come together to redeem the gains of their independence struggle by creating a just and democratic society.

Given the gravity of the situation at this historical juncture, as difficult as it may be, Eritreans must find ways and avenues of amalgamating resources so that they may rescue their country and people from the grip of tyranny in ways that are democratic and enduring.

As we write this book, we are aware that there is no way of knowing the future. Nor can we predict the full range of political developments possible in Eritrea between now and the next few years. But we can consider a few realistic scenarios for discussion and reflection about the country's possible future. One is the real possibility of the Eritrean army taking state power through violent means. This has been suggested many times and, in fact, unsuccessfully attempted at least once in recent years. If comparable histories of other African states that have suffered postcolonial totalitarianism(s) and ended up in military coups can provide a lesson, it is that this should not have come as a surprise in the first place (as it did in some corners), and should not come as a surprise if it happens again. Likewise, Eritrea would be no exception to the negative long-term consequences of a potential military coup. The problem with military takeovers is that, once established, the new leaders often tend to engender more violence, replicating the mistakes of the dictators they overthrew and wanting to convert their initial role of "reformers" into permanent "rulers". Another possibility is that despite the widespread socio-economic and political discontent of people inside the country and in the diaspora, the ruling elite might find ways and means to continue governing the country for a very long time. The well-being and role of the president will be critical here. Yet another opportunity to be explored is the avenue of national reconciliation as a transition toward, as formulated in the first chapter of this book by Awet Weldemichael, "a participatory political system governed by the rule of law". In order for the process of national reconciliation to succeed, however, it must embrace "all threads of the social, cultural, political, and historical fabrics that constitute Eritrea". The success or failure of such a venture ultimately will depend on the willingness of the ruling elite – or influential elements within the group – to seek a negotiated settlement to the ending of their monopoly on power. Most importantly, it will require a mature handling of the situation and leadership from opposition groups with the ability to garner sufficient political clout to exert the necessary pressure.

A fourth, and most radical, scenario is the replacement of the regime by an incumbent people's movement or popular uprising to change the system with a popular and democratic structure of governance. With no clear signs of open public resistance at present in the form of civil protest and disobedience as witnessed during the Arab Spring, it is true that the realization of this scenario is more hypothetical than the other scenarios. Yet, the possibility cannot be summarily dismissed. Should such a prospect arise involving the most oppressed agents of society standing up against their oppressors, it would be the most desired venue for Eritrea's transformation into a democratic and sovereign state, precisely because the gains would be driven and protected by the interests of the people who effected the democratic agenda for change. Nonetheless, change cannot be achieved by merely wishing to dismantle the present structures of the ruling political order. They must go hand in hand with a deep desire and commitment to not repeat the mistakes of the past. For this to happen, any movement that contends with power to build the country must do so on the basis of a "National Constitution" whose principles enshrine the genuine wishes and diverse aspirations of the pluralistic aspects (linguistic, ethnic, religious, class, and gender) of the society. The future leaders must also seriously ask and reflect on hard questions regarding Eritrea's political identity and cultural ideology. The significance of the history of the hijacked revolution of Eritrea under the guise of "exceptionalism" is that it nearly always has served, as it continues to do so today, to deceive the country and the people, with its leaders claiming that the country is doing exceptionally well even when it is doing outstandingly badly. It will be necessary for the future leaders of the country thus to ponder on questions such as "Who are we?", "Who are we not?", and "Who, then, Do We Desire to Be?".

These questions need to be examined in relation to ourselves as a people and country, and in relation to the African continent. Raising and reflecting on such questions is important especially when Eritreans and their country, as in the present, are characterized by paranoia, alienation, and a profound sense of melancholy imposed upon them by a domestic violence perpetuated by a monstrously paranoid, alienating, and alienated political system. If they take that journey of self-reflection and self-definition, the next generation of the country's leaders and their constituencies may learn that the real challenge for them and their people is not to ask whether they are "special" or their culture "exceptional". Rather, the challenge is to understand and accept that in fact all humans, countries, and cultures share similar values of which Eritreans can be a part, and by which they can thrive together as a people and nation in dignified peace with the rest of Africa and the global community of nations and peoples.

Bibliography

"Gaudium Et Spes: Pastoral Constitution on the Church in the Modern World." *La Santa Sede*. December 7, 1965. Last accessed August 1, 2017. http://www.vatican.va/archive/hist_councils/ii_vatican_council/documents/vat-ii_cons_19651207_ gaudium-et-spes_en.html.

"Mater Et Magistra: Encyclical of Pope John XXIII on Christianity and Social Progress." *La Santa Sede*. May 15, 1961. Last accessed August 1, 2017. http://www.vatican.va/holy_fathe r/john_xxiii/encyclicals/documents/hf_j-xxiii_enc_1505196 1_mater_en.html.

"Quadragesimo Anno: Encyclical of Pope Pius XI on Reconstruction of Social Order." *The Holy See*. 1931. Last accessed August 1, 2017. http://www.vatican.va/holy_father/pius_xi /encyclicals/documents/hf_p-xi_enc_19310515_quadrage simo-anno_en.html.

"Rerum Novarum: Encyclical of Pope Leo XIII on Capital and Labor." *La Santa Sede*. 1891. Last accessed August 1, 2017. http://www.vatican.va/holy_father/leo_xiii/encyclicals/doc uments/hf_l-xiii_enc_15051891_rerum-novarum_en.html.

Ammar, Wolde-Yesus. *Eritrea: Root Causes of War and Refugees*. Baghdad: Sinbad Printing Press, 1992.

Arendt, Hanna. *On Violence*. San Diego: Harcourt Brace & Company, 1970.

Asmerom, Ghidewon Abay. "መሰረት ህዝብን ሃገርን ንምድዋን ብሽም ሃይማኖት ዝግበር ዘሎ ፍንፉንን ርኹስን ጠቓናዊ ጎስጓስ፡" speech delivered in Washington, DC, December 8, 2013. Available at: https://www.youtube.com/watch?v= HML4d OqXorc (last accessed on August 1, 2017).

Berryman, Philip. *Liberation Theology*. Philadelphia: Temple University Press, 1987.

Cantalupo, Charles and Ghirmai Negash. *Who Needs a Story?: Contemporary Eritrean Poetry in Tigrinya, Tigre, and Arabic.* Asmara: Hidri Publishers, 2005.

Carson, Donald A. "Reflections on Salvation and Justification in the New Testament." *Journal of the Evangelical Theological Society* 40, no. 4 (1997), 581.

Catholic Bishops of Eritrea, *Making God's Ways Straight: Pastoral Letters and Documents (1991 – 2007).* Bologna: Editrice Missionaria Italiana, 2008. The entire book and individual messages/documents within it are translated from the Tigrinya originals in the same publication as ካቶሊካዊያን ጳጳሳት ኤርትራ, *መንገድታቱ አቅንዑ: ሓዋርያዊ መልእኽታትን ሰነዳትን (1991– 2007).* Bologna: Editrice Missionaria Italiana, 2008.

Césaire, Aimé. *Discourse on Colonialism.* Monthly Review Press, 2000.

Connell, Dan. "Eritrea: Enough! A Critique of Eritrea's Post-Liberation Politics." *allAfrica.com.* November 6, 2003. Last accessed August 1, 2017. http://www.danconnell.net/sites/default/files/Enough-A%20critique.pdf.

Connell, Dan. "Inside the EPLF: The Origins of the People's Party & its Role in the Liberation of Eritrea." *Review of African Political Economy* 28, no. 89 (2001), 345-364.

Connell, Dan. *Conversations with Eritrean Political Prisoners.* Trenton, NJ: Red Sea, 2005.

Creary, Nicholas M, editor. *African Intellectuals and Decolonization.* Athens: Ohio University Press, 2012.

De Tocqueville, Alexis. *Old Regime and the French Revolution.* Translated by Stuart Gilbert. New York: Dover Publications, 1955.

De Waal, Alexander, editor. *Demilitarizing the Mind: African Agendas for Peace and Security.* Trenton, NJ: Africa World Press, 2002.

Deriu, M. "Una rivoluzione de ll'immaginario." *Obiettivo decrescita.* Editrice Missionari Italiana, Bologna, 2008.

Dodson, Michael. "Liberation Theology and Christian Radicalism in Contemporary Latin America." *Journal of Latin American Studies* 11, no. 01 (1979), 203-222.

Döring, Tobias. "Christine Matzke." In *African Cultures, Visual Arts, and the Museum: Sights, Sites of Creativity and Conflict.* Amsterdam [u.a.]: Rodopi, 2002.

Douglass, Frederick. "If there is no Struggle, There is no Progress." *BlackPast.org.* August 3, 1857. Last accessed August 1, 2017.

http://www.blackpast.org/1857-frederick-douglass-if-there-no-struggle-there-no-progress#sthash.IIyScRxi.dpuf.

Fanon, Frantz. *The Wretched of the Earth*. Translated by Richard Philcox. New York: Grove Press, 2004.

Fessehatzion, Tekie. "Is the Cease-fire Holding? Barely, But That's Not Bad Considering..." *Dehai News*. July 25, 2000. Last accessed August 1, 2017. http://www.dehai.org/conflict/articles/tekie_Cease-fire_Holding_Barely.html.

Foroohar, Manzar. "Liberation Theology: The Response of Latin American Catholics to Socioeconomic Problems." *Latin American Perspectives* 13, no. 3 (1986), 37-57.

Gooren, Henri. "Catholic and Non-Catholic Theologies of Liberation: Poverty, Self-Improvement, and Ethics Among Small-Scale Entrepreneurs in Guatemala City." *Journal for the Scientific Study of Religion* 41, no. 1 (2002), 29-45.

Grinker, Roy Richard, Stephen C. Lubkemann, and Christopher Burghard Steiner. *Perspectives on Africa: A Reader in Culture, History, and Representation*. John Wiley & Sons, 2010.

Guevara, Ernesto "Che". *Guerrilla Warfare*. Lanham: Scholarly Resources Inc., 1997.

Gutiérrez, Gustavo. *A Theology of Liberation: History, Politics and Salvation*. Maryknoll NY: Orbis Books, 1973.

Habtemariam, Semere T. "Pastoral Letter: A Complete and Literal Translation." *Awate.com*. June 19, 2014. Last accessed August 1, 2017. http://awate.com/pastoral-letter-a-complete-and-literal-translation/.

Hailu, Gebreyesus. *The Conscript: A Novel of Libya's Anticolonial War*. Trans. Ghirmai Negash. Athens, Ohio: Ohio University Press, 2013.

Hochschild, Adam. *King Leopold's Ghost: A Story of Greed, Terror, and Heroism in Colonial Africa*. Houghton Mifflin Harcourt, NY: Pan Books, 1999.

International Commission on Intervention and State Sovereignty (ICISS), *Responsibility to Protect* (Ottawa: the International Development Research Centre 2001). Last accessed on August 1, 2017: http://responsibilitytoprotect.org/ICISS %20Report.pdf.

Iyob, Ruth. "The Eritrean Experiment: A Cautious Pragmatism?" *The Journal of Modern African Studies* 35, no. 4 (1997), 647-673.

Juana, Alvaro de. "Archbishop Romero had no Interest in Liberation Theology, Says Secretary." *Catholic News Agency*. February 21,

2015. Last accessed August 1, 2017. http://www.Catholic newsagency.com/news/archbishop-romero-had-no-interest-in-liberation-theology-says-secretary-79788.

Kingsley, Patrick. "It's not at War, but up to 3% of its People Have Fled. What is going on in Eritrea?" *The Guardian.* July 22, 2015. Last accessed August 1, 2017. https://www.theguardian. com/world/2015/jul/22/eritrea-migrants-child-soldier-fled-what-is-going.

Latin American Bishops. "Poverty of the Church." *Povertystudies.org.* September 6, 1968. Last accessed August 1, 2017. http:// www.povertystudies.org/TeachingPages/EDS_PDFs4WEB /Medellin%20Document-%20Poverty%20of%20the%20 Church.pdf.

Levine, Daniel H. "Assessing the Impacts of Liberation Theology in Latin America." *The Review of Politics* 50, no. 02 (1988), 241-263.

Lewis, Clive Staples. *God in the Dock: Essays on Theology and Ethics.* Grand Rapids, Michigan: William. B. Eerdmans Publishing, 2014.

Magubane, Bernard. *The Ties that Bind: African-American Consciousness of Africa.* Trenton, N.J.: Africa World Press, 1994.

Makki, Fouad. "Nationalism, State Formation and the Public Sphere: Eritrea 1991–96." *Review of African Political Economy* 23, no. 70 (1996), 475-497.

Mamdani, Mahmood. *When Victims Become Killers: Colonialism, Nativism, and the Genocide in Rwanda.* Princeton and Oxford: Princeton University Press, 2001.

Mazrui, Ali A. "Seek ye First the Political Kingdom," 105-126. In Mazrui (ed.) *General History of Africa, Volume VIII: Africa Since 1935.* James Currey, University of California Press, and UNESCO 1999.

Mbembe, Achille. *Critique of Black Reason.* Translated by Laurent Dubois. Durham and London: Duke University Press, 2017.

Mbembe, Achille. *On the Postcolony.* Berkeley: University of California Press, 2001.

Mesfin, Dawit. *Woldeab Woldemariam: A Visionary Eritrean Patriot, A Biography.* Trenton, NJ: The Red Sea Press, 2017.

Miglierini, Julian. "El Salvador Marks Archbishop Oscar Romero's Murder." *BBC News.* March 24, 2010. Last accessed August 1, 2017. http://news.bbc.co.uk/2/hi/8580840.stm.

Negash, Ghirmai. "The Freedom of the Writer." *Warscapes*. Last accessed August 4, 2017. http://www.warscapes.com/retro spectives/eritrea/freedom-writer.

Negash, Ghirmai. *A History of Tigrinya Literature in Eritrea*. Leiden: CNWS-University of Leiden, 1999.

Ranger, Terence. "The Invention of Tradition in Colonial Africa." In *Perspectives on Africa: A Reader in Culture, History, and Representation*, edited by Roy G. Richard and Christopher B. Steiner, 597-612. Cambridge: Blackwell, 1997.

Ratzinger, Cardinal Joseph. "Liberation Theology." *Christendom Awake Website*. August 6, 1984. Last accessed August 1, 2017. http://www.christendom-awake.org/pages/ratzinger/liberationtheol.htm.

Ratzinger, Joseph Cardinal. "Instruction on Certain Aspects of the 'Theology of Liberation'." *La Santa Sede*. December 9, 2004. Last accessed August 1, 2017. http://www.vatican.va/roman_curia/congregations/cfaith/documents/rc_con_cfait h_doc_19840806_theology-liberation_en.html.

Schmidt, Elizabeth. *Foreign Intervention in Africa: From the Cold War to the War on Terror*. Cambridge: Cambridge University Press, 2013.

Selassie, Bereket H. *Wounded Nation: How a Once Promising Eritrea Was Betrayed and Its Future Compromised*. Trenton, NJ and Asmara: the Red Sea Press, 2010.

Smith, Christian. *The Emergence of Liberation Theology: Radical Religion and Social Movement Theory*. Chicago: University of Chicago Press, 1991.

Tawfeeq, Sheikh. *YouTube*. April 12, 2014. https://www.youtube.com/watch?v=j28fIc6yciI.

Tesfai, Alemseged. *Two Weeks in the Trenches: Reminiscences of Childhood and War in Eritrea*. Trenton, NJ: Africa World Press, 2002.

Tronvoll, Kjetil, and Daniel Rezene Mekonnen. *The African Garrison State: Human Rights and Political Development in Eritrea*. Rochester, NY: James Currey, 2014.

Venosa, Joseph L. *Paths Toward the Nation: Islam, Community, and Early Nationalist Mobilization in Eritrea, 1941-1961*. Athens: Ohio University Press, 2014.

Welde Giorgis, Andebrhan. *Eritrea at a Crossroads: A Narrative of Triumph, Betrayal and Hope*. Houston: Strategic Book Publishing, 2014.

Weldemichael, Awet Tewelde. *Third World Colonialism and Strategies of Liberation: Eritrea and East Timor Compared.* New York: Cambridge University Press, 2013.

Weldemichael, Awet T. "African Diplomacy of Liberation: the Case of Eritrea's Search for an 'African India'." *Cahiers d'Études africaines,* Vol. 4, No. 212 (2013/4), 867-894.

White, Aaronette M. "All the Men Are Fighting for Freedom, All the Women Are Mourning Their Men, but Some of Us Carried Guns: A Raced-Gendered Analysis of Fanon's Psychological Perspectives on War." *Signs,* Vol. 32, No. 4 (Summer 2007), 857-884.

Woldemikael, Tekle M. "Eritrea's Identity as a Cultural Crossroads." In *Race and Nation: Ethnic Systems in the Modern World,* edited by Paul R. Spickard, 350. New York and London: Routledge, 2005.

Wrong, Michela. *I Didn't Do it for You: How the World Betrayed a Small African Nation.* HarperCollins Publishers, 2005.

Wrong, Michela. *In the Footsteps of Mr. Kurtz: Living on the Brink of Disaster in Mobutu's Congo.* New York: HarperCollins Publishers, 2001.

Younis, Saleh AA. "PFDJ Should Dissolve Itself." *News.Asmarino.Com.* July 2001. Last accessed August 1, 2017. http://fp.asma rino.com/Comments/July2001/Saleh_Younis_07-03.asp.

Zere, Abraham T. "Review of Kab Rix' Ḥafnti, by Tekie Beyene." *Journal of Eritrean Studies* 6, no. 1 (2012), 149-156.

Appendix

Translated from the original Tigrinya text into English by Semere Habtemariam and, with his permission, reproduced here verbatim.

"Where is your brother?" (Gen 4:9)
Pastoral Letter of the Catholic Eparches of Eritrea, Easter (2014), Asmera, Eritrea

Semere Habtemariam (trans.), 19 June 2014:
http://awate.com/pastoral-letter-a-complete-and-literal-translation/
(Last accessed October 21, 2017)

Greetings:
1. From God our Father and our Lord Jesus Christ; to the faithful who are "our children in faith", to all people with good wills, may His Grace, Mercy and Peace be with you. Through Christ's Resurrection victory over sin and death was achieved; and on this age of Resurrection, where you live in light by the Lord; and wear the fruit of light which consists in all goodness, righteousness and truth (Eph 5:8-9), we express our good wishes.

Beloved brothers-and-sisters-in-Christ:

"Faith is the substance of things we hoped for and the evidence that we will realize them; one that helps us understand of things not seen as if they are seen," but also one which explains "that the worlds were framed by the word of God," and that through the light of faith we understand the meaning and message of all things which happen and come (Heb 11:1-3), and it is on the basis of this faith that we have taken it upon ourselves to present you this Apostolic message.

Gratitude:
2. At a time when a lot of people have departed from the faith because of the deception of wrong understanding, we think of, "your work produced by faith, your labor promoted by love, and your endurance inspired by hope in

our Lord Jesus Christ" (1 Thess 1:3). We always thank God for all of you and continually mention you in our prayers (1 Thess 1:2).

"The light of faith to illumine our human experience from within, accompanying the men and women of our time on their journey…showed how faith enriches life in all its dimensions…" (Light of Faith by Pope Francis); we should then deliberate on the Year of Faith, guided by the Word of God, and these are our considerations and conclusions.

We have started the Year of Faith with much success of spiritual renewal; assessed for an entire year the overall state of our faith, our journey of faith; we were able to praise and sing to God, pray and confess; and earlier we were blessed to inaugurate the Eparchy of Segeneyti which was a significant step in the history of our church, and hereby extend to God our utmost gratitude in the unshakable faith He bestowed on those who preceded us.

Objective:

3. In his message "Door of Faith," Pope Benedict XVI had advised the Church and those of us who shepherd the faithful and his words are pertinent because they duly reflect the realities of our times. "The Church as a whole and all her Pastors, like Christ, must set out to lead people out of the desert, towards the place of life…towards the One who gives us life, and life in abundance." Furthermore, "It often happens that Christians are more concerned for the social, cultural and political consequences of their commitment, continuing to think of the faith as a self-evident presupposition for life in society. In reality, not only can this presupposition no longer be taken for granted, but it is often openly denied. Whereas in the past it was possible to recognize a unitary cultural matric, broadly accepted in its appeal to the content of the faith and the values inspired by it, today this no longer seems to be the case in large swathes of society, because of a profound crisis of faith that has affected many people" (Door of faith by Pope Benedict XVI)

4. It is in light of these enormous challenges; and to strengthen our faith, that our holy father, Pope Benedict XVI has prepared for us the Year of Faith. Saint Paul advises his disciple Timothy to 'aim at faith' (II Tim 2:22) with the same constancy as when he was a boy (II Tim 3:15). And we, the Catholic bishops of Eritrea, hear this invitation directed to each of us, have the duty to awaken people, that none of us, the faithful brothers and sisters, grow lazy in the faith.

Beloved brothers and sisters: We assure you that "we have prayed for you because such an important "faith may not fail" (Lk 22:32). Christ on the eve of his passion told Peter to strengthen his brothers and sisters in the same faith and we need to understand that the same applies to us. God went looking for man, "where are you?" (Gen 3:9); and likewise, our father, Pope Francis, in his last address asks us, "Where is your brother?" (Gen 4:9). In order to look after the well-being of our brother, "which is helping us to sense the great joy of believing and to renew our wonder at the vast horizons which faith opens up, so as then to profess that faith in its unity and integrity, faithful to the memory of the Lord and sustained by his presence and by the working of the Holy spirit" (Light of Faith by Pope Francis). This is what prompted us to write this; or objective.

Part II: Considerations/Conclusions of Year of Faith

What is Faith?

5. Inspired by the Year of faith we just celebrated, desiring to reach newer heights and march on through a renewed life; we conducted these deliberations/considerations. The Year of Faith has been concluded means that it signifies that we will continue our journey aided by the new strength we have acquired; it does not mean that the true year of Faith has ended; but that it has started and that it will continue.

It is therefore important that we realize how much joy faith gives one; the faithful person, the faithful people; and how the unfaithful differs; the advantages of believing in God; and how not believing is the greatest harm one can incur on oneself.

The person who does not believe in God is one who does not have a sense of the origin of the world and one's place in it; and lacks direction and purpose in life. The unfaithful believes the world came into being through chance and accident, but the faithful believes it was created by God; fruit of his omnipotence, love and goodness; and it is a great gift given to us to live in it responsibly.

6. Without faith, the injustices, affliction and suffering will pass on as such, and the victim will be subject to pity; but with faith God will wipe every tear from their eyes (Lk 22:32) and heal their wounds. And all the people will see God's salvation (LK3:6).

If it is without faith, then the best of life's experiences such as goodness, love, comity, friendship, mercy, mutual support, philanthropy…will be meaningless and transient. But with God, whether it is at the beginning or at the end, there will always be goodness and love. In everything we do, we will be encouraged and strengthened by Jesus Christ himself who is the alpha and omega of love.

If it happens to be without love, then death is the end of all, and it will sever all ties of human relationships. With faith, however, death will be our departure from this temporary world; and entrance to a life with God; where we will unite with those who preceded us in heaven that does not have an end.

7. When we think without faith, then, we will succumb into thinking that we are here as a result of chance or accidents; our destiny will be meaningless and untrustworthy, our fate will be determined by the hands of the few powerful and subjected to damnation. When we have faith in God, we will understand that we are here because of the God who created the earth and heavens, we will care about our brother, and eventually we will return to the home prepared for us by our Father, even when our lives are marked by temporary setbacks, strife and hardships; at the end of all, we know that we have God's grace—His guarantee. Everything "that is not sweetened by Christ remains sour and bitter," (St. Bernard) by faith, and particularly the belief in Christ, "I am the way and the truth and the life" (Jn 14:6) which will guide and light our lives. Life without faith is falling in the abyss of darkness. "If you do not stand firm in your faith, you will not stand at all" (Is 7:9).

8. When we say the faith revealed by Jesus Christ is the victory that has overcome the world (Jn 5:4), we do not mean to despise our world or to isolate ourselves from its affairs, but to open our hearts and go beyond the known cantors and enter into a covenant with God to achieve a wholesome life full of joy; and know that we can defeat arrogance, ill-intentions, hatred and sin. It is to underscore that with faith, man made in the likeness of God; a child of God; must live loving each-other under one Father; looking after the well-being of their brother and sister. This is because… "man was created not to die; indeed, God created him in his image for everlasting life" (The Wisdom of Solomon 2:23); and God as always has not ceased asking "Where is your brother?"

"…man will continually be under the spirit of God; and cannot ignore the question of faith; all experiences of the past as well as the present attest to this very fact. As always man longs and strives, although not in the right way, to understand the meaning and the secrets of his life, works and death…" (Joy and Hope, 2nd Vatican Council). There is a big difference between knowing Christ and not knowing him; to journey with his company or to travel blind-folded without him; to head his words…to be with Jesus is to have a life enriched with the spirit; and to be able find meaning in everything…" (Joy of the Gospel, Pope Francis)

9. The Church has the responsibility to shed light with the Gospel on the temporal and worldly affairs (18). Because "The joys and the hopes, the griefs and the anxieties of the men of this age, these are the joys and hopes, the griefs and anxieties of the Church…" "The light of faith is not to make us forget the suffering of this world," but it is faith "that will guide us in the steps we take, and light that is needed in our journey." Because Christ, who is the alpha and omega of our faith, wants us, in his light, to partake in his vision came looking for us, "Adam, where are you?" (Gen 3:9) Based on the faith,

"that nourishes our lives daily and strengthens and encourages us anew;" it is our duty to consider our situation and the situation of our brother.

We embark on this task, not because we are interested in gaining worldly or temporal honor or faith, or to bring others into our fold, but by a genuine desire to serve (22). In embarking on this undertaking our faith has a lot to do with it. "An authentic faith—which is never comfortable or completely personal—always involves a deep desire to change the world, to transmit values, to leave this earth somehow better than we found it" (The Joy of the Gospel by Pope Francis) is what helps us.

10. To see the light of faith means to receive "the great gift brought by Jesus" (Light of Faith by Pope Francis 1). "In God's gift of faith, a supernatural infused virtue, we realize that a great love has been offered us, a good word has been spoken to us, and that when we welcome that word, Jesus Christ the Word made flesh, the Holy Spirit transforms us, lights up our way to the future and enables us joyfully to advance along that way on wings of hope. Thus wonderfully interwoven, faith, hope and charity are the driving force of the Christian life as it advances towards full communion with God (Light of Faith by Pope Francis 7). It is therefore important to realize that "this road which faith opens before us…is the origin of this powerful light which brightens the journey of a successful and fruitful life" (Light of Faith by Pope Francis 7).

11. "…Men expect from the various religions answers to the unsolved riddles of the human condition, which today, even as in former times, deeply stir the hearts of men: What is man? What is the meaning, the aim of our life? What is moral good, what is sin? Whence suffering and what purpose does it serve? Which is the road to true happiness? What are death, judgment and retribution after death? What, finally, is that ultimate inexpressible mystery which encompasses our existence: whence do we come, and where are we going?…"(2nd Vatican Council) "…By contrast, when a divine instruction and the hope of life eternal are wanting, man's dignity is most grievously lacerated, as current events often attest; riddles of life and death, of guilt and of grief go unsolved with the frequent result that men succumb to despair" (Hope and Joy, 2nd Vatican Council). This is the biggest tragedy of all.

Part III: Current state of Affairs

God's blessings
12. Seeing from the perspective of where we have been, it is important that we remember that we have benefited from the blessings of our God. Although our country does not have an over-flowing abundance of natural wealth; compared to other countries that suffer from natural calamities, it has been blessed by calm and peaceful weather; and more importantly, by God-

fearing and peace-loving people who value harmonious coexistence and who shun any kind of ethnic, religious or partisan confrontations; where the various kinds of differences and diversities are seen as a blessing; where focus is patiently and calmly placed on the bright future on the horizon; and by people who believe in peace; and for that we are greatly grateful to God.

The base or source of all of these is because our people have deeply-rooted and long-standing faith. This faith is what had enabled and enabling our people to live harmoniously with each-other, with God and themselves. From long ago, our people have internalized the moral question of "Where is your brother?" (Gen 4:9) and have unfailingly responded in the affirmative with fraternal care by sharing each-others happiness and sadness, good and bad times; they have never responded in the negative, "I don't know! Am I my brother's keeper?" (Gen 4:9). In order not to lose our peoples' value system of faith, but to strengthen it; we call upon you in our prayers, Lord, to increase our faith.

Although we have tried to put several projects of development in place in order to move forward, because in life it is natural to think of advancing ahead, and to look from a distance at those destinations we have not been able to reach; and because it is impossible to hide wounds that have not healed yet; we should not be deceived by those positive outcomes only and ignore the negative ones. This is a reflection of every aspect of our lives; it affects our psychological and emotional feelings, our collective civil life; our life in its entirety for it encompasses our spiritual and moral dimensions. "It is up to the Christian communities to analyze with objectivity the situation which is proper to their own country" (Joy of the Gospel, 184)

Those who perished in the sea
13. "A voice is heard in Ramah, weeping and great mourning, Rachel weeping for her children and refusing to be comforted, because they are no more" (Mt 2:17-18 & Jer 31:15). In the last months of September and October, the season of harvest and the renewal of life, where the hope of the New Year of our Geez calendar inspires us all; our people with the rest of the world were shocked and shaken by the tragedy that has snatched the lives of many of our youth who drowned in the Mediterranean. This tragedy was the culmination of all the suffering that has been inflicted by human traffickers, smugglers and human oppressors in the past years, in every mountain, valley, desert and sea. It is therefore very important that we take stock of the current and previous tragedies.

The whole people mourned their death together in public and not in their private homes. "…All night long she cries; tears run down her cheeks…the young women who sang there suffer, and the priests can only groan" (Lm 1:2-4). This is because those who went out in search of good have fallen victims to suffering and destruction; and it is in the recognition of what transpired in the times of the prophet Jeremiah that the Old Testament words were quoted. Likewise, Matthew the Evangelist, has put the same thing in the New Testament.

The Old Testament reminds us of the event that took place in Jerusalem and vicinity in 587 B.C., when the invading Babylonians forced the people of Jerusalem to leave their city for Ramah (today's Ramallah), and then burned it down. They then took the children of Jerusalem as captives, therefore from now on, "they were not." In that time, we are told that Rachel, the one who represented the people and mothers of Israel, and was the mother of Israel, cried. The prophet did not forget the hope of returning home, but to underscore how much the whole country and people were affected by their loss.

14. By remembering the tomb of Rachel in Bethlehem the Evangelist Matthew draws a parallel with the death King Herod inflicted on the children. He said "they are all dead" to signify that Rachel, in the name of all mothers, was not comforted when she cried; the crying and wailing will reach God and God is the only comforter; this is not in private words only but with the hope of resurrection when the dead will be risen and comforted. The words, "They are dead; they are no longer there" will be changed; their crying and wailing will cease; and the suffering that had befallen them will be remedied with their resurrection.

Events like this: drowning in the sea, death in the desert, suffering at the hands of human-traffickers, happening in our advanced times, on the door-steps of the so-called developed countries is truly "shameful and unacceptable, and does not go with the developments and advancements man has made" admonished Pope Francis.

In solidarity with Rachel, mother of all, and with all the mothers we send our tears and prayers to God. In faith, we pray for our children, who in search of a good life perished in the tragedy they faced, to gain comfort, which had eluded them in this world, in the bosom of God; and to enjoy the good life that no one can take away from them, in His presence. And to the parents and relatives who miss their departed children, who, by not been able to bury them have not found any closure; we extend our condolences and pray that the God who comforted Job will likewise comfort you.

Refugee Exodus
15. While we let our departed children seek comfort in His bosom, God will come and ask us, "Where is your brother? Where is your sister? Where is/are your child/children? What is the condition in which they find themselves?..."

This loss and devastation has been going on for years now, but God will ask, those of us who have made a habit of chit-chatting about these tragedies, questions which will make us worrisome and stressful (Joy of the Gospel, 211). When the question of "Who is responsible for this?" is raised; and everyone gives one's account and the truth is told, there will be an occasion where the hierarchy of responsibilities and roles will be invoked. But in general and most important terms, the source of these tragedies is long and wide that concerns all of us. This question will naturally force us into asking "How is our country doing? What kind of conditions do we find it in…? We cannot hide behind, "Am I my brother's keeper?" anymore.

• Parents who, for selfish reasons, wed their children to those who come from abroad without doing their due diligence.

- Parents have developed this blind view that their lot will only get better if their children leave the country regardless they are adults or minor. They believe that once their children are out of the country they will be taken care of and don't have to do much…

- Instead of working hard to better our living standards inside the country, it has become the norm to think that going into exile is the way to achieve better opportunities.

- For how long are we going to let the search for better life abroad continue? Why it is that all the efforts and counseling have not produced the desired result, and particularly in light of the fact that the illegal journey is much too costly? If what has been tried has failed, why can't we try other better approaches?

- As a sign of the times, some are fleeing their country; and it can be said like the proverb, "Most calves (btey in Tigrinya is younger than a calf) play around not as a result of being well-fed but because they see other calves playing around;" the majority of our youth are, however, in a situation "where they could not envision a better life; where they could not plan for the future; where they could not start at one point to reach another; where they could bear current hardships to reach a desired and sought after destination; where they could not hope for anything…" This is the source of the problem.

- It is possible to raise the question, "Is the no-war-no-peace" responsible for this predicament? But does it also mean that we don't have the will or the ability to change the status quo? What can be done to change the situation that is adversely affecting our country and people? The solution lies within us; if the international community fails to shoulder its responsibility, the victim has the imperative of self-interest to work hard and seek solution to one's problems. The current predicament only benefits those who oppress/exploit people and the traffickers and smugglers, and not the people and the country; and hence, it is obligatory to see ways to get out of the no-war-no-peace situation.

Because we have failed to change the status quo, life has become unbearable; and lured by the wealth beyond our borders and a life one knows nothing about, the change-seeker youth ventures on the journey; and in the beginning it was conducted through legal and proper channels, but now it has completely gone awry, and the youth have become victims of the high seas and wild beasts and the inhumane human and organ trafficking; and this has reached very troubling proportions.

16. In the wilderness it is natural for beasts to be hostile to man. What is troubling is, however, the emergence of a phenomenon where people are kidnapped while seeking refuge and taken hostage for lucrative ransom; man has become man's worst enemy; man, who has been created in the image of God, has been deprived of his dignity and rights when his organs are harvested to be sold in a black market. We have never heard of anything like this in history; when one sees the time of slavery and rule of the beasts making it in our advanced world; one is bound to ask if the conscience of the perpetrators has been desensitized, why it is that the world that is witnessing this is so tolerant? Why not the rush to condemn and confront it; particularly those places this inhumane and barbaric acts are taking place and those people who are committing the crime; and on those these things are committed under their watch…governments and leaders should not have spared any effort to thwart it!! Is it because our will has waned that this shocking practice is allowed to continue? Or our ability has been emasculated? Or if there is any exerted effort, is it because it has not borne any fruit? Or who is benefiting from this? What can we say? If above all things, this cannot escape the judgment of God, it is still important that history and time render its judgment and make the truth known to all.

Many have noted and given their recommendation that to change the status quo, it will require a massive coordinated effort, a change in our thinking, and a fundamental change in the way we practice work and conduct business. It also compels you to consider and raise fundamental questions and demands through the legal and political process; failing to shoulder this responsibility will make us accountable in front of God and our fellow-man. "For we must all appear before the judgment seat of Christ, so that each of us may receive what is due us for the things done while in the body, whether good or bad" (2 Cor 5:10).

"When the order of values is jumbled and bad is mixed with the good, individuals and groups pay heed solely to their own interests, and not to those of others. Thus it happens that the world ceases to be a place of true brotherhood. In our own day, the magnified power of humanity threatens to destroy the race itself" (Joy and Hope, 2nd Vatican Council, 37).

The Affairs of our life

17. It is easy to notice that our people are enduring many wounds. Poverty, hardships associated with diseases such as HIV AIDS, going into exile and its concomitant problems that brings death to some, misery to the living; while we say may the dead inherit the kingdom of God; we pray and ask God to give us strength to address, in the spirit of unity and harmony, the past and prevailing current issues that concern us.

Our land is turning into desert; its productivity and wealth is being eroded. To strengthen all efforts of preservation or renewal, a public campaign must be waged to increase public awareness. This is because, according to Pope Francis, God "has called us to be stewards of the environment and keepers of our brother;" for the environment and brother we take care of, will take care of us in return.

As the saying goes, "console the one who died hit by lightning with fire," our country is not only being betrayed by the land, the most serious problem confronting her is the refugee exodus.

- The youth are fleeing the country either to pursue their education abroad or after finishing their education; and hence the country is being depleted of its educated and young generation.
- Children accompanied by their mothers are following the parent who has already fled the country, and also in search of better opportunities.
- Even elder parents go abroad, presumably, to see their children and grand-children and while there they are seeking asylum and upon being granted they don't return home.

It is therefore clear that the country is becoming poor in terms of its human capital, as evident in any social setting; it is not only the youth but also the so-called middle generation who are fleeing the country; it makes you wonder what will be the fate of a nation that loses its youth and its main source of power? It is people who make a country and beautify a country; and without people it simply will not be a country.

18. We are obliged to say this because it is happening right in front of our eyes; and we are duly concerned by the far-reaching ramifications the continual exodus of refugees and the depletion of human capital will incur on the future of the country. It is true wherever a refugee settles s/he will always miss and long for his/her homeland; but truth be told that based on history the number of those who returned home is insignificant to merit counting. We are not only talking about the youth and the middle generation, but also about those infants and children who either join them or are born in their adopted country; we are afraid all these are net loss for our country.

As the saying goes, "Getting used to has more impact than giving birth to;" and the children and grand-children of the ones who have mentioned above will have the culture and identity of the places they were brought up in; and unless an effective campaign of instilling in them the love of their culture, country and people is waged; it will prove to be another problematic loss. But a country can only be built by those who stay inside to build it. Our country is hearing a cry of its depletion and bareness. Her cry is to everybody: to individual families, village elders, religious leaders, and political leaders...; it is an appeal. For the sake of those remaining not to leave, for the sake of those who have left to return, we need to undertake tasks that will reflect courage and creativity.

19. Are we to say that our father's saying, "one can never get tired of one's eyes and country" is forgotten? The disposition and thinking of today seems to say to the contrary, "a country is where one is comfortable," meaning that wherever comfort and the good life is, that should be one's country. If this is the case then, it is necessary to exert all efforts and explore all creative means to make this country give its people or try to give them comfort, the joy of work, the good life, peace, and security. The prevailing conditions compel us to repeat what the Church has said in 2001, "There is no point in saying why our youth are focusing on going abroad. When we have a country full of peace, justice, work, freedom of expression, a country one could make a living in; there is no one who has honey who goes looking for one; we will have our youth who do not long to go abroad, but we will have those who have left return home. The country was made for the people; and it is evident that people were not made for the country.

Psychological Conditions
20. In light of what has been aforementioned and the prevailing conditions that have proven to be anathema to the dignity of human life; people have become skeptical of the prospects of the future and are asking, "What guarantee do I have?" Because we have not been able to find answer to this question, ignoring the dignity of human life has become the norm. Regardless of the means, our preoccupation has become of how to take advantage of any situation and profiteering; but we have to be aware that this cannot bring solution to our problems. People have not been able to reach what they hope for, gain what they wish for, realize what they dream for, and achieve what they worked for; and the resultant frustration and stress have become the normal.

Everything rewarding endeavor and system is beyond our borders; there is nothing useful in our country...etc. have become so widespread. These prevailing conditions have clouded our blue sky. Instead of working hard to make a good and decent living inside the country, the majority are consumed by the thought of getting out.

In conjunction with all of these, many factors such as family members being confined in the army under national service, reconstruction projects and prisons; lack of care-takers of aging parents have caused great emotional stress upon all. It is obvious the kind of harm it will cause a family when its most productive members are taken away from it. We should not just look at the economic harm this causes; it is not hard to understand the psychological, emotional and moral crisis that come to all those who stay home behind and those who live isolated from their families. It is not without a reason that the number of stress-related diseases such as blood pressure, cholesterol, heart attack and psychological problems have risen dramatically.

Social Conditions
21. Our customary and normal way of social life is slowly becoming a thing of the past; the pillar that holds our social life is been uprooted and we can say that we are heading toward utter collapse where there is no return or a remedy for it (Jer 4:11-21).

The Family Condition
Whether it is due to the impact of modern mass media or the prevailing situation the times have incurred on the youth, the respect for parents and village elders; and the influence and responsibility they have on their children and younger generation has not only waned but seems to disappear all-together. We say to them, even if you feel your place and respect in society has been undermined, you should not give in; don't surrender. Now more than ever, we urge you to lead by example; to walk the path of reconciliation and mediation; not to be misled by temporary comforts and luxuries; to look beyond the horizons for things to come; and to save the families. The salvation of the families is the salvation of the nation. The question of "Where is your brother?" specifically applies to the family and what goes on in the family; for it is the family that give rise to brotherhood, and the place where it is allowed to grow and blossom. The family is the cornerstone of the church.

We have neither quietly listened to our brother nor reached an agreement; we have not paid attention to the well-being of our brother by asking, "Where are you? Where is s/he?"; we have not taken the initiative to understand what others are saying and doing; and in consequence our differences and problems are growing by the day.

Moral Upbringing and Edification
22. In the area of public and communitarian administration; it has been forgotten that power is from the people and to the people, and that those in authority are there to serve the public; and hence favoritism and nepotism

and feathering one's own nest in both legal and illegal means have become the norm; to reverse and restore this situation to its rightful place will require creativity, responsibility and commitment to doing the right thing. It cannot be denied that the word "corruption" itself will imprint scars and incur damage in our social life.

What is meant by corruption in not only the monetary greasing of the palms in order to obtain things one deserves or not; but to go beyond societal, legal and moral norms and customs, and engage in activities that are not acceptable by community standards. It can be seen that the root-cause of this is the poor oversight, and the failure to introduce transparency and accountability; not speaking up and exposing corruption and focusing on only what is in one's selfish interest; as a result, corruption has become a lake where many have drowned. Extreme corruption is when one utterly disregards the truth and embraces falsehood in life's journey. One who does not have a fear of God and respect for His laws will certainly find himself in situations where injustice and transgressions are present. "With one accord they too had broken the yoke and torn off the bonds" (Jer 5:1-11).

How do we get out of this mess? The disease of corruption has taken root because it was not nipped in its bud. In terms of spiritual leadership, the moral edification of a person is a long journey that starts with a proper upbringing; and one that will require a comprehensive moral and spiritual campaign of revitalization; and where the political and civic systems built on transparency and good policy-making, and the strong institutionalization of legal administration cannot be delayed.

Rule of Law
23. One of the essential characteristics of our people is their awareness of the supremacy of the rule of law. One who invokes "In the name of the law" is feared more than the one who carries a rod or a weapon of war because the rod of the law is as strong and as straight as a man standing erect. Is it because we have forsaken this beautiful tradition that we have been overwhelmed by rampant corruption? Or is it corruption that is causing its death? People have to be aware of this because it has an enormous impact on their development and the development of the country. All those who are imprisoned or taken into custody must be treated, first and foremost, in humane and compassionate way, and then to charged and have their day in court in a reasonably quick manner so justice can be served; but most important of all, we need to demand a constitutional rule of the county and all justice and fairness-minded people must give it their utmost attention because it is the foundation of our true unity.

Not being able to engage in public discourse or dialogue about the important issues and challenges facing the country in writing or verbally; lack of information and transparency; ignorance about issues that concern the nation; and lack of clear understanding; has led to succumbing to hearsay, falsehood and rumors; and the spread and dominance of a mentality that says, "Why should I care?"

It can be seen that our problems and differences are growing by the day because we have failed to listen to the voice of our brother and reach an understanding; we did not look after the well-being of our brother by asking where is he and where are you; and we did not take the initiative to understand the situation and points of view of others.

Education
24. Education is the foundation of work and development; and if it is to be the springboard for societal change; if we desire the new generation to transform the country; then we need to fundamentally reform our educational system through creative approaches. If the young generation are to learn with an open and free mind, then there must be a future of opportunity they can compete for and visualize from afar. It is education that has enabled the developed countries to enjoy many blessings; and if we want to achieve similar accomplishments, then it is clear that we need to adopt and embrace their time-tested and well-proven innovative and creative systems.

Considering humanity as a whole and what has been developed and accepted by all as human values such as truth, brotherhood, freedom, equality, democracy, justice and fairness, rights and legitimacy, accountability and so forth, the Church can play an important role in education by promoting these fundamental principles. In order to achieve these objectives, it is necessary that we follow what has been tested and proven by history; it is good to learn from the experience of others.

"The social order requires constant improvement. It must be founded on truth, built on justice and animated by love; in freedom it should grow every day toward a more humane balance. An improvement in attitudes and abundant changes in society will have to take place if these objectives are to be gained" (Joy and Hope, 2nd Vatican Council, 26).

The Economy and Living Conditions
25. If we look at every household or family from an economic perspective, certain questions come to mind: What would have happened if there were no near and distant relatives living abroad? How could families manage without the Diaspora support? We are here reminded by the wisdom of our fathers who say, "God creates a precipice with mountain climbing stairs on it." But this cannot be a lasting solution. If we cannot create jobs; if the fresh-blood youth are not allowed to pursue rewarding occupations of their choice; if we cannot reignite reconstruction works and commerce; then we should know

that the many wounds and diseases will be exacerbated by the grinding poverty and inevitably lead to paralysis. We need to liberate ourselves from foreign dependency; if this holds true for the nation; it is also equally pertinent to individuals and individual families (except those with disabilities and unable to take care of themselves). But this can only be realized through the promotion of work, and not by words, however beautiful they might be.

In addition to the rising cost of living, inadequate earnings, home rents that increase daily; lack of employment in an occupation of choice; for example, the construction sector, which used to employ many and diverse sectors, has come to a standstill; and all have consequently incurred an adverse impact on our society. If we cannot move and work freely; if we cannot earn a living through our own sweats, if individual and peoples' freedom are not strengthened; how it is that we can understand the freedom of a nation? And where we can find it? In brief, integral human development and work presupposes free choice and creativity of the individual and of peoples if it is to be meaningful and dignifying for no structure can guarantee their development over and above human responsibility (Caritas in Veritate 17).

This is not about luxuries and comforts; but about what determines our survival and non-survival, like our daily bread, water, light and other basic necessities. Since these are the fundamental basic needs, they deserve utmost attention by those responsible authorities. In brief, the economic system has to be planned with the sole objective of serving the people.

The Moral/Ethical and Spiritual Life
26. When we come to the moral and spiritual dimension of our lives; it makes us wonder if our delicate and deep wounds will ever heal again. When we look at our moral and spiritual life with focus, we find a situation that makes us ask, "Are we the same people? Have we changed? And have we become different? Our moral principles and ethical practices have changed; what were once a part of us have completely vanished; and new ones are thriving in their place instead; but our morality is the true reflection of our identity; and our situation bear testimony to that. It looks like what Saint Paul had said is coming to pass, "people will be lovers of themselves, lovers of money, boastful, proud, abusive, disobedient to their parents, ungrateful, unholy, unloving to their parents, irreconcilable…and without self-control" (2 Tim 3:2). In this manner, Satan-worship makes its way; and it is important to remind people that it comes in the name of advancement. We cannot hesitate to say that there are Satan-worshipers among us.

"Unlike former days, the denial of God or of religion, or the abandoning of them, are no longer unusual and individual occurrences. For today it is not rare for such things to be presented as requirements of scientific progress or of a certain new humanism" (Joy and Hope, 2nd Vatican Council 7).

There are a few who regard religious faith as an appendage; and not guidance for life, and a standard by which morality is judged; and even worse use faith to feather their own nests; preach while ignoring the Cross and crucifixion. This is the wrong path. Religious faith cultivates peoples' spirit and morals; and leads them to better and higher growth, reconciliation and harmony, and peace and satisfaction in life.

27. The portrayal of religious faith as a source of division, without any positive contribution, and with harmful and negative consequences can be understood as an integral part of the ongoing spirit of treason and betrayal that is causing great harm to our country and our people. To the contrary, because the question of faith greatly contributes to identity, harmonious coexistence and nationalism; a society that does not take a clear stand on the issue of faith or straighten her relationship with God can never achieve worthy accomplishments.

On the other hand, faith empowers people to engage in dialogues, and good relationships; and encourages them to foster harmonious coexistence with those who are different from them. When one expects others to respect his/her faith; it is incumbent upon him/her not to attack or criticize the faith of others; for this concerns justice. The fruit of good and true faith is dialogue, engagement, rapprochement, and mutual understanding. The person who does not want to be part of this kind of mutual understanding, of quietly listening to and sharing ideas with others, or of receiving feedback and constructive criticism in transparency can only be one who suffers from lack of self-confidence.

28. In conjunction with all these, we also have many instances that show that our understanding of money and how it should be earned has completely changed. We have made money the measurement of everything; and we are pursuing its acquisition by all means (Machiavellian rule). Whether in commerce and trading activities; in (business and governmental) offices; those landlords who rent homes...we see that they have all become slaves to money and worshippers of money; amassing money in illegal and immoral, ways without any qualms, as if it is the norm. It is now clear to everyone, that this kind of cupidity and selfishness, is what has led to the organ and human trafficking that has shaken and shocked the entire world.

Since the worship of money is a form of idolatry; it will lead to where humans and their organs will be trafficked; and females will sell their bodies in degrading markets. The only thing that will save us from the sin of idolatry is the true spirit of faith. "But godliness with contentment is great gain. For we brought nothing into the world, and we can take nothing out of it" (1 Tim 6:6-7). And Jesus said, "No one can serve two masters. Either you will hate the one and love the other, or you will be devoted to the one and despise the other. You cannot serve both God and money" (Mt 6:24).

The Root-cause of Our Wounds and Problems
29. Our wounds that don't seem to heal; their deep and delicate source, and what makes them revisit us, is the sin that dwells in man. If we asked how this is explained? It is the life that is lacking in love, care and sympathy; which is manifesting in many ways in the form of selfishness and the widespread feeling of I shouldn't care as long as I am doing well. The cupidity, selfishness, moral corruption and irresponsibility that is circulating in all aspects of life has incurred on the people and country un-healing wound; and this will inevitably lead to a life devoid of unity and to a dangerous situation. If we ask, "Who is responsible for all of these?", there will certainly be varying levels, but there is no one who can claim innocence; "If we claim to be without sin, we deceive ourselves and the truth is not in us" (1Jn 1:8).

A child was asked to put together the mixed pieces of a puzzle that make the map of the world. The child noticed that there was a picture of a man on the back of the board. He started separating noses and ears…and shortly was able to make the image of the person; while simultaneously solving the map puzzle on the front side; he achieved double victory. The moral of the story is that in order to reform the world man must reform himself first.

If human endeavors are to succeed, whether at the national or individual level; if it is to be balanced, honorable and dignified; if it is to be, in brief, a wholesome experience; then there has to be a strong foundation that will support a systemic structure where God is at the top and man right below him. "Unless the Lord builds the house, the builders labor in vain" (Ps 127:1) A country is not just a piece of real estate; but people with shared experience of making a living, and history of life's journey; people who have received in unison the good and the bad; hot and cold; and the good and the evil; people who made advances together with one goal and who solidified their bond through interconnectedness. We can therefore call a national journey good and right if it primarily considered man and his problems, and his prevailing and past historical conditions.

The Journey for Peace
30. In the previous section, No. 12, we remembered that we have "peaceful people who live in peace;" and it was right to see it as a blessing and good; but "…when we say peace, it does not only mean the absence of war; it is not a peace as a result of a balance of power among competing sides; it is not also a peace that comes due to a hegemonic or an all-powerful tyrannical system. When we say peace, we mean the "enterprise of justice and fairness" (Isaiah 32) that is conducted through proper and right means. For this purpose, it is rooted in the internal peace and calmness structured into a human being by

its Maker. Peace ensures that everyone enjoys due rights; and rights and privileges are conferred through legal means; if this peace is to come, it has to be rooted in the internal peace given by God, who structured the society; and by those people who thirst for justice and always on the move to make it a reality. (Peace and Joy, 2nd Vatican Council 78).

Peace falls in jeopardy when transgressions and injustices are let to blossom; and when jealousy, arrogance and mistrust reign supreme. The foundations of peace disappear when any man's rights and dignity are undermined, and is deprived of what is rightfully his. We don't say, "justice delayed is justice denied" for nothing; but because it makes a strong foundation for peace, and it is for this why we need to expedite the dispensation of justice for those who are waiting for it, for those who are been sought by the law, and for those who are already in custody. The projects of peace and justice go hand in hand in harmony like strings of music, and cannot be separated. The situation has become where we truly see and hear the one who raised the troubling question, "Where is your brother?"; his echo, cries and tears, "appealing to God from the ground" (Gen 4:10).

Conclusions
In this period of Resurrection when we commemorate and honor the risen Christ; when our country celebrates its 23 year independence-day anniversary, we pray to God to bless our country; so it can be reborn and rise again, a country of love and hope; to make it a country of justice and fairness; we all have an obligation to pray and work hard: religious leaders, people and individuals. We believe that all believers and people of good will in this country will pray for peace, dialogue and understanding. On the basis of what Christ told us, "I will do whatever you ask in my name" (Jn 14:13) we believe our prayers will not be in vain. It is clear therefore that our country is thirsty for the peace that will come from God. "Peace I leave with you; my peace I give you. I do not give to you as the world gives. Do not let your hearts be troubled and do not be afraid" (Jn 14: 27).

Pat III: Witness
"You will be my witnesses" (Acts 1:8)

31. "If once the flame of faith dies out, all other lights begin to dim, and the light of faith has to be lit again" (Light of Faith, 4). To ensure that the flames of faith are always waving, the light of faith is always lit means and nothing else but only that the prophesized words will be fulfilled and witnessing will be highly valued for, "you will be my witness in Jerusalem, and in all Judea and Samaria, and to the ends of the earth" (Acts 1:8).

These strong and powerful words of Jesus are being said to us today. In the beginning these were said to his followers; the community of faith started to grow. The Church is still growing. We recognize that we have a role to play in this ongoing growth; and know that we are an integral piece and parcel of it. Those who carried the weight of these mentioned words such as Abune Selama (Saint Frumentius) and those who preceded and followed the Nine Saints planted the seed of Christianity in our country and made it grow. This was followed later on by Abune Yacob Guistino who preached to strengthen the foundation of Christianity and to give her a renewed awareness; it is clear that we live today enjoying the fruit of their labor and what was built by them and their followers and successors. By observing the sign of the times and by responding to the demands of each time, the Church, over the course of time, has devised projects according to its regulations and today in our county the Catholic segment of our population have four eparchies as they continue their journey.

32. To all those who led and worked in the field of faith; who journeyed back and forth in faith, and all the bishops, priests, monks, nuns and faithful parents who bequeathed us the faith, we remember them in gratitude. The Catholic faith has taken root; it is a Church that continues the works performed by Christ and the words preached Him through its broad based education projects, health services for the sick, orphanages, human development projects that specially cater to women and are easily available and the preaching of the Gospel. Today the Church honors and continues its witnessing by combining philanthropy and evangelism, for it gives great weight to the question, "Where is my brother?" Today, it is true that the segment of the faithful who should inherit the faith, especially the young generation who has spread and gone in all countries; and live in situations which are hostile to their faith; and this is greatly troubling.

We should not be misled by the spirit of saying we are okay; like weak creatures we should believe that we carry the burden of our limitations, human inadequacies and sins; but without any despair and hopelessness we should seek refuge in the grace of God. In this journey, the first step is to wear the spirit of confession. We should believe in our limitations and deficiencies; we should not shy away from forgiving those who trespass against us; and not retaliate against those who do us harm.

33. The Christian journey in general; and the demand for reform the journey of the Year of Faith makes; we should confront it with many approaches; first and foremost what kind of direct relation we have with God, the Father, with His son, Jesus Christ, our Savior, and with the Holy Spirit, giver of life? How is the life of the faithful and the faithful life? This is the time where we need to look into the state of our faith and the society we live in from the perspective of the brother we care and love. "There are ecclesial structures which hamper efforts at evangelization, yet even good structures are only helpful when there is a life constantly driving, sustaining and assessing them.

Without new life and an authentic evangelical spirit, without the Church's fidelity to her own calling, any new structure will soon prove ineffective" (Joy of the Gospel).

34. If we look at what Jesus has given us in the Bible in parables and his own and his disciples' life examples, it is that the small seed of the divine kingdom will grow to bear fruits, but will have to die first; this is Christianity's rule and steps of development; and because of this we should never, as individuals and community despair by what we encounter but find encouragement in it. We should say like Saint Paul, "When I am weak, then I am strong" (2 Cor 12:10). "Do not be afraid, little flock, for your Father has been pleased to give you the kingdom" (Lk 12:32).

We need to look into the future journey and stage; we should remember the guiding words spoken at the opening session of the 2nd Vatican Council by the recently canonized, by the Vatican Council and the whole Church, His holiness Pope John XXIII. "Our duty is to earnestly and fearlessly dedicate ourselves to the work that needs to be done in this modern age of ours, pursuing the path which the Church has followed for almost twenty centuries (Pope John XXIII, opening remarks). The main mission of the Church is to faithfully and with enthusiastic creativity continue spreading and deepening the work of evangelism. In order to do our evangelical work, we believe that the Holy Spirit which worked through the apostles and awakened their listeners will arm (cloth) us with ability, desire, will and courage (Pope John XXIII, opening remarks).

How can we be able to honor our witnessing? By being reconcilers, forgivers and followers of the path of peace; do not conform to this world (Rm 12:2), live with the spirit of Christ, and fulfill your obligations from the perspective of your fellow-man. "In loyalty to their country and in faithful fulfillment of their civic obligations Catholics should feel themselves obliged to promote the true common good. Thus they should make the weight of their opinion felt in order that the civil authority may act with justice and that legislation may conform to moral precepts and the common good" (Apostle Message and Faith, 2nd Vatican Council).

The fact that the Church herself, meaning her leaders and members must follow confessions is attested by the words of the prophet Jeremiah, "If you repent, I will restore you that you may serve me...you will be my spokesman. Let the people turn to you" (Jer 15:19).

Preaching the Gospel
35. When we look into our future journey, we immediately notice the priorities of our Church's mission. We have learned necessary lessons and made important observations from our past experience; all based on the

Gospel we inherited; and made catechism and liturgy the center of our lives. All these have been duly integrated into our daily lives. All that needs to be done have been listed in the following document: 1. The Council's document titled, "To the People"; 2. "Preaching the Gospel Today" by Paul VI, 1975; 3. "Christ's Mission" declaring the canonization of his holiness John-Paul II; 4. The Synod of Bishops of 7-28 October, 2012, on new evangelization; and 5. "Joy of the Gospel" by Pope Francis.

We have to remind all faithful that if our country is going to be a true witness to Christ, then, it is a journey we should all take. When people say evangelism, what is meant is to preach in His name, since Christ is the Savior of the world. We, Christians, should preach the encouraging and empowering message of mercy and salvation "in season or out of season" (2 Tim 4:2) because that is the greatest contribution we can offer the country. The message is to inspire hope and love, as the Word of God tells in the Holy Book; for its fruits dwells in the mysteries of life; as it is always honored and remembered in liturgy, and life bears testimony to it. This kind of evangelism requires the spiritual participation (campaign) of all people of God.

Christian in name only
36. One of the issues the 2nd Vatican Council addressed with great concern is the phenomenon that has been called, "The Nominal Christian." In its Council declaration titled, "Joy and Hope," section 43, "Many people have not been able to reconcile the faith they profess with their daily lives; and this split between the two deserves to be counted among the more serious errors of our age." Who are the nominal Christians? Those who are not concerned with their faith; who do not see their faith as guidance for their life; who do not worship God, their Savior, with their fellow Christians; those who selectively embrace parts of their faith and ignore others; in general, we recognize the nominal Christian by these attributes: He is one who has been baptized but has not active participation in his Christian community; a Christian who is hibernating in cold weather and his life lacks warmth and energy. "Although baptized, their life does not reflect the obligations of baptism" (Joy of the Gospel, 15). "Dear children, let us not love with words or speech but with actions and in truth" (1 Jn 3:18)

37. For all of these and generally for everything else, we need new evangelism. In his 1973 Latin American address, Paul VI, defined "New Evangelism" as evangelism that is pursued with a "new enthusiastic spirit, creativity, interpretation and approach." In consideration of the new changes in a society, the Church needs to adopt new language, new way of teaching, new way of evangelizing and new way of life; and a new king of witnessing.

We need to reach out to the ones who have left the Church; and those who have stopped coming to church and bring them into the fold of faith. We need to go in the direction of those who are spiritually poor, those who are thirsty and hungry for God; and those who are Christian but who live as un-Christians and refuse to come to church. Every person in his heart of hearts and intrinsic conscience has feelings for God; meaning that each person has "a heart within the heart" that is God; and it is for this reason that one cannot be fully satisfied without God (Saint Augustine).

38. In this type of evangelism, there is a call to all children of the Church to actively participate as disciples; there is a need to make the necessary arrangements, projects and a solid ground where they can serve; in brief, the faithful lay must be aware of the roles they can play in the fellowship and unity of the Church; in this way it is necessary to empower and energize their participation, and we should all be preached to and preach. The Church can succeed in teaching and passing on the contents of the faith if it connects its Gospel teaching with daily lives of the faithful. What makes the Gospel spread is not an intellectual enquiry, but the witness the faithful bear in works and living. "The faithful should guide their life journey with love; give life to faith; and express it in charity and in their works as best they can. They should all bear in mind that they can reach all men and contribute to the salvation of the whole world through public worship and prayer as well as by penance and voluntary acceptance of the labors and hardships of life whereby they become like the suffering Christ" (Apostolic Message, 16). In carrying out their apostolic works, the faithful will be joined by their leaders, the bishops and monks at the frontlines, who have committed their life to Christ.

What is weakening/undermining our Faith?
a) The spirit of the world and secularism

39. Saint Paul strongly reprimanded those who went astray from the spirit of Christianity and fell for various inclination, "I am astonished that you are so quickly deserting him who called you in the grace of Christ and are turning to a different gospel," (Gal 1:6). The words of Saint Paul speak to us today because our life and culture does not reflect the spirit of Christ but the spirit of the world; we have made virtue of vices such as fortune-telling (spiritism, mediums, the occult and psychics), fornication, falsehood, theft, bribery, adultery and are no longer shocked by it or ashamed of it. The excessive love of money and selfishness that we have mentioned earlier; being consumed by frequent pursuit of temporary carnal pleasures; and the abdication of morality and the Christian way of life in the pursuit of money and wealth...; the source of all of these ills is, "religious ignorance or indifference; the preoccupation with the cares and riches of this world; the bad example believers set and the problems it creates as a result; and the modern ideas that are very hostile to faith" (Catechism of CC, 29).

In brief, the one who believes in temporary luxury, wealth and comforts (materialism), does not think of the future and his thinking and disposition is devoid of spirit. He does not consider God, and according to the author, George Elliot, he is someone who is not deeply aware, but one who is fully downed in his egoism; and thinks and acts only in terms of "I can take care of me"; putting himself in God's place; making himself the source of life instead of God; promoting the mentality of if I have money, I have everything else; and this is what is distancing many from God. There is a cause for fear that this might make it in the Church. When the trusted egoism, money and the world leave, the person who knowingly closed his heart to God will be left in limbo; and to the contrary, the one who believes in the meaninglessness of these and approaches God in need and empty handed, his heart will be filled. Because God's mercy is limitless.

"Do you not know that the unrighteous will not inherit the kingdom of God? Do not be deceived: neither the sexually immoral, nor idolaters, nor adulterers, nor men who practice homosexuality, nor thieves nor the greedy nor drunkards nor slanderers nor swindlers will inherit the kingdom of God" (1 Cor 6:9)

b) Not enough Christian cultivation

40. "Always be prepared to give an answer to everyone who asks you to give the reason for the hope that you have. But do this with gentleness and respect" (1 Pt. 3:15). In order to respond in either words or action, one must first have the maturity and understanding that is necessary; the knowledge of the teachings of the faith, partaking in sacraments—mysteries of faith; but above all the witness one bears through Christian dedication. In the grand scheme of things and understanding, it is clear that we should struggle to eliminate the ignorance of faith. The age of innocence and good times, when one was able to live with what was learned in one's childhood, is long gone. "In the present historical conditions in which man finds himself, he faces great difficulty in trying to know God by the light of reason alone" (Catechism of CC, 37-38). In order to confront the challenges of these trying times, it is necessary to have a strong spiritual revivalism.

What Strengthens Faith?
a) Unshakable Faith in God's Providence

41. According to 2 Pete 3:18 which says "Grow in the grace and knowledge of our Lord and Savior Jesus Christ"; we need to lead our lives in his grace and knowledge. What is meant by unshakable faith is that God provides for and supports those who are with him; and for this reason we should only rely on the One God and not on those we think they have the power or ability of fortune-telling; because it is not permitted by our faith. When we seek God

with our concerns and aspirations, it should not be "my needs have to be met," but to live reassured by faith and God's providence.

As is often the case, we will be faced where our faith in God's providence will be tested. When the help you prayed for is delayed or when you feel that your prayers are not heard by God, be aware that faith is not transactional but one that will require patience and steadfastness. "All forms of divination…conjuring up the dead…consulting horoscopes and astrology, palm reading, interpretation of omens and lots…and recourse to mediums and other practices from God's perspective contradict the honour, respect, and loving fear that we owe Him" (Catechism of CC, 2116).

b) To Be Faithfull to Christ's Church

42. The true follower of Christ accepts "All of Christ"; meaning he accepts the head and the rest of the body; and because of this, it is wrong to say "Yes, to Christ" and "No, to the Church." We need to follow the Church and accept its teachings on faith and make her a part of our life—individual and communitarian. When we heed and follow the teaching and commandments of the Church, it means we have arranged a guarantee for our righteous and balanced life of faith.

c) Carrying the Cross of Christ

43. "… The Cross of Christ represents God's love for the world; the evidence that He is the source of all grace; and that the Church has the duty and responsibility to preach it…" (NA, 4). Following Christ means the readiness for the obligation to carry his cross. "Whoever wants to be my disciple must deny themselves and take up theirs cross and follow me" (Mt. 16:24). There is a direct correlation between our faith and dedication to the Church of Christ and our willingness and readiness to carry his cross. To accept the cross of Christ is to accept God's plan without any despair and hopelessness in life; and it empowers us to wait with patience and steadfastness. For this reason, our life of faith must be one of a covenant characterized by priestly service, dedication; and readiness to carry and preach the cross of Christ. Because Christianity is the seed that grew to fruition on the cross; to be on the side of the cross to bear testimony that a Christian is firmly rooted in his faith, and one that assures and sustains the power of his faith.

d) Developing the habit of reading the word of God—the Bible

44. "Man shall not live on bead alone" (Lk 4:4). "The days are coming when I will send a famine through the land, not a famine of good or a thirst for water, but a famine of hearing the words of the Lord" (Amos 8:11). One of the wishes and aspirations of the Year-of-the-Faith is the fulfillment of the

words of the Prophet Amos; for the people of God to have the burning desire and eagerness for the word of God and for this to be imprinted in their hearts; for their lives to be revitalized with by the word of God that they eagerly embrace and read.

In its "Word of God" declaration, the 2nd Vatican Council has said and it is our hope that, "the life of the Church is invigorated and strengthened by partaking in the sacramental celebration of the Eucharistic mystery, and similarly we hope for the spiritual revitalization of life on the basis of the special reverence and spirituality we have for the word of God, which "lasts forever" (Is. 40:8; see 1 P. 1:23-25)" (Dei Verbum, 26). The word of God has come to us through him and because "not knowing the Holy Book is to not know Christ" (St. Hieronymus/St. Jerome), the priests and pastors of the people of God must work hard to continue the structured reading and knowledge of the Sacred Scripture.

Those who give the reading of the Sacred Scripture its utmost attention are the faithful and those, who in full awareness, study it. We urge that the constant and structured reading and understanding of the Bible be based on the teachings and interpretations of the Church. What assists in this endeavour is the presence of many published holy books that are translated in various languages, and this is great blessing. It is important that these are done in the right and proper way, if the reading of the word of God is to have a fruitful and revitalizing effect.

e) Partaking in Sacraments (the mysteries of life)

45. "Just as she venerates the body (flesh and blood) of Christ, the Church has always venerated the sacred Scriptures …unceasingly receiving and offering to the faithful the bread of life from the table—both of God's word and of Christ's body" (Word of God, 2nd Vatican Council, 21). Since the Eucharist is "… the fount and apex of the whole Christian life" (Lumen Gentium, 11). "Come to me, all you who are weary and burdened, and I will give you rest" (Mt 11:28). "No Christian community, however, is built up unless it has its basis and centre in the celebration of the most Holy Eucharist" (Decree on the Ministry and Life of Priests, 6). In our tradition, this spiritual honour and respect has been held at the highest regard. This must receive special consideration on the mysteries of Christian life; a Christian life that experienced fatigue must be renewed to gain its main courage and strength; to know that this is available in the mysteries of life and that we should be rooted in it and nourished by it; this is what the Year of Faith asks of us.

If the readiness and commitment of the faithful to participate in the Holy Eucharist is to be a huge step forward, then we have to ensure that they do so in the right and proper way, and believe that our situations and lives will be renewed by the grace of Christ's sacrifice. The fruit and outcome of this will be evident when we experience it in our daily lives; by frequently engaging ourselves in conciliatory and forgiveness activities; purifying ourselves through the Sacrament of Penance; and nourishing our lives by receiving the Holy Communion. We are called upon to protect, preserve and cherish the Sacrament of the Holy Matrimony for it is the foundation of the family and the reflection of a true union. In times of sickness and death, we need to conduct ourselves in the right way, according to the Sacrament of Anointing of the Sick, for we wear a Christian life that is necessary and right.

f) With Mary at the Cross: Children of Hope and Resurrection

46. O members of God's people whom we love with all our hearts; we urge you to follow, with courage and steadfastness, the footsteps of the Virgin Mary, who has been named "the Star of Hope," in faith, hope and love; and to be like "...those who persevered the present time and made the most of the opportunity with faith and hope" (EP 5:16; Col4:5) "and who patiently wait for the honor that has yet to come" (Rom 8:25). It means you have demonstrated you are the children of hope.

We urge not to conceal this hope inside your hearts, but to continually make it shine in your daily lives in this world and live it with faith and courage. You have to continually come to God and confess; and fight with courage (Light of People, 2nd Vatican Council) "against the rulers, against the authorities, against the powers of this dark world and against the spiritual forces of evil" (Eph 6:12).

Conclusion
As faithful Christians and your belief in the Gospel, you should take solace from glad tidings of the Good News; and follow the Church-like mother of Jesus, Mary, who, in hurry went to visit her relative, Elizabeth, in the highlands of Judea; to give this world hope; by steadfastly bearing the burden; because you should know that you have been called to travel the roads of history (Saved by Hope, Pope Benedict, 50). For faith to remain solid like a rock; for hope to be vigorous and vibrant; for love not to get cold, we urge you to live in Christian courage, bear witness, and enjoy the grace of God. "In all our prayers for all of you, we pray with joy" (Phil 1:4).

To rise with Christ means to change oneself through an internal journey of confession and penance; because it transforms one from darkness into light; if we are not able to be the children of light, we will not be able to see the truth; and we do not have the truth, it means we are not free (Jn 8:32). May you be lit by the light of the resurrection; may you be filled by the light of resurrection; to be qualified and credible witnesses; may the God of Peace, who made us rejoice with the resurrection of his Son, grant you his peace and serenity.

(Prayer)
O our mother, Mary "… Thus you remain in the midst of the disciples as their Mother, as the Mother of hope…teaches us to believe, to hope, to love with you. Show us the way to his Kingdom! Star of the Sea, shine upon us and guide us on our way…" (Saved by Hope, Pope Benedict, 50)

"O Star of the new evangelization, that the joy of the Gospel may reach to the ends of the earth, so the fringes of our world will be illuminated, help us to bear radiant witness to communion, service, ardent and generous faith, justice and love of the poor. O mother of the Living Gospel! Wellspring of happiness for God's little ones, pray for us. Amen. Alleluia! (Joy of the Gospel, 288).

Catholic Bishops of Eritrea

Signed by:
Abune Mengishteab Tesfamariam, Eparchy of Asmera
Abune Thomas Osman, Eparchy of Barentu
Abune Kidane Yebio, Eparchy of Keren
Abune Fqremariam Hagos, Eparchy of Segeneyti.

Index